DECEIVING
TROUT

Published by Stoeger Publishing Company
55 Ruta Court
South Hackensack, New Jersey 07606

ISBN 0-88317-141-4

Published by arrangement with SeTo/Halcyon Publishing,
Auckland, New Zealand

Distributed to the trade by Stoeger Industries
55 Ruta Court
South Hackensack, New Jersey 07606

In Canada, distributed to the trade by Stoeger Canada Ltd.,
Unit 16, 1801 Wentworth Street

P.O. Box 445, Whitby, Ontario L1N 5S4

Printed in Hong Kong through Colorcraft Ltd.

DECEIVING TROUT
THE FLYTIER'S ART

Text and Photographs by
John Parsons

Flies tied by
John Morton and Brian Hussey

STOEGER

ACKNOWLEDGEMENTS

This book would not have been so pleasurable in the making, or so deeply researched, without the extensive flyfishing knowledge and literary resources of Bryn Hammond, of Kingfisher Books, Taupo, who identified scores of source-books and placed them at my disposal. I am deeply grateful to him for his help, advice, and comments.

To John Morton and Brian Hussey I offer my warmest congratulations and thanks for the series of exquisite flies tied for the book. I hope my photographs do them justice.

My thanks are also due to Dr D.J. Forsyth of Taupo for reading the manuscript and steering it clear of entomological pitfalls, and to Alex Gillett of Greytown and Brian Hussey of Taupo for advice and comment, and lending newly published source books.

John Morton tied: the Muddler Minnow, chapter 2; the Greenwell's Glory, chapter 3; the Coch y Bonddu, chapter 11; the Pye's Sedge, chapter 12; the Ant, chapter 16; the Morton's Annie, chapter 17; the Shrimp, chapter 19; the Water Boatman, chapter 21; the Craig's Night-time, chapter 22; the Green Beetle, chapter 24; and the Mouse, chapter 25.

Brian Hussey tied: the Grasshopper, chapter 1; the Woolly Worm, chapter 4; the Cicada, chapter 5; the Quill Gordon, chapter 6; the Damselfly Nymph, chapter 7; the Midge Pupa, chapter 8; the Sawyer's Pheasant Tail, chapter 9; the Smelt, chapter 10; the Palmer, chapter 13; the Kakahi Queen, chapter 14; the Caddis, chapter 15; the Smut, chapter 18; the Snail, chapter 20; and the Spider, chapter 23.

INTRODUCTION

Three special truths illuminate this book. First, the universality of the food forms taken by trout; second, the wisdom of carrying imitations of them all; and third, the value of the portmanteau pattern.

Those truths are not of my making. They emerge from any reading of trout-fishing literature from several countries. So many food forms throughout the world of trout are virtually the same everywhere. Imitations of one form developed in one country will deceive trout just as readily in another.

Again and again in the millions of pages devoted to flyfishing for trout, anglers lament their lack of an imitation to match the particular natural that trout are avidly taking at the time. Nothing can be more frustrating.

Unfortunately, unless like Dr Mottram you carry a fly-tying wallet with you and can fashion something on the spot, you can't remedy the situation until the next occasion, when hopefully the fly-box will display two or three copies of a new addition tied up at home in the meantime. The newcomer may well qualify as a portmanteau pattern, embodying the characteristics of two or three naturals, rather than just one, commonly taken by trout.

The 25 food forms and imitations studied in the following pages will go most of the way towards an understanding of what the trout eats and how best to imitate it. It doesn't go all the way. Trout take more food items than just 25, but not often. True, I have included a mouse, and mice are not exactly a staple food, so why not frogs, millipedes, wasps, click-beetles? Ah well, we could go on and on.

Three other matters deserve the attention of flyfishers keen to offer close imitations of natural food forms to the trout they fish for. All three make for more enjoyable fishing, and not necessarily because they bring more fish to the fly.

First, get to know what aquatic and terrestrial foods are available to your trout, and when. Second, study as many of those foods as you can, ideally at regular intervals through the season, noting sizes, colour changes, shapes, silhouettes, and the specific movements that bring those foods to the notice of the trout. Third, base your imitations on those characteristics, paying particular attention to colour, shape, and size and, when you're fishing them, to bringing movement to them typical of the movement of the naturals.

Even so, don't get too carried away by the exact-imitation syndrome. It's wonderfully rewarding, certainly, to fish a pattern representative of a specific natural being taken by trout and to have fish unhesitatingly accept it. But much of the time we just can't say what is being taken. Provided we know what is available we can make a pretty shrewd guess, but few trout are totally selective, particularly in stillwaters, and they will just as readily take one food item as another.

So, on the other hand, yes, make a thoroughly serious study of the foods available and use appropriate imitations accordingly. On the other hand, enjoy the fun of experimentation and inexactitude. Absolute knowledge of trout and trout foods implacably applied denies you that 'glorious uncertainty' which is so satisfying. It might even bring on fits of uncontrollable rage when fish insist on gobbling something well outside our meticulous expectations. And that would never do.

CONTENTS

1
NOT QUITE
CRICKET

Ernest Hemingway wrote the finest American fishing story I have ever read. *Big Two-Hearted River* enshrines in just 8,000 words exactly the kind of fishing and the kind of country and the kind of writing I like. They bring me back to that unforgettable story of the 1920s time and time again.

All the same, I know about Ernest's son Jack's disenchantment with the river and its setting years later. And I know what Robert Traver instinctively knew about the story and the disguises in which the author had protectively dressed the place and the trout that had made such magic for him.

But I don't think about Jack Hemingway's disillusionment or Traver's uncannily perceptive study. I'm travelling with Nick and his heavy pack across burned-over country, seeing with him that first pathetic grasshopper of the story, victim of the black-ash aftermath of the fire; and later fishing healthier grasshoppers with him to the big trout downstream.

G.E. Mannering, a generation before Hemingway, like many another New Zealander of the time, fished live grasshoppers no less enthusiastically. At Makotuku, one of his favourite places on the Manawatu, usually with his friend W.H. Galwey, he used to do extraordinarily well. At his first attempt with the grasshopper he landed five nice fish. Much of the fun of grasshopper fishing, he recalled, lay in first catching your bait; a sentiment expressed by William Senior, 20 years earlier, from Bothwell, on Tasmania's Clyde river, where the locals wielded long-handled butterfly-nets and admitted that catching the grasshoppers was frequently the most exciting phase of the trout-fishing there.

Grasshopper fishing goes back much further than Senior. Flyfishers must have used the naturals for centuries, casting them downstream and upstream, dapping them through bankside foliage, tripping them across the waves on blowlines billowing from drifting boats on breezy lakes and lochs.

We shall never know who tied the first artificial, but in 1651 Thomas Barker advised imitating the green grasshopper, and 25 years later Charles Cotton was describing the dressings for a green grasshopper and a dun grasshopper, both to be used in June.

Mind you, it's quite obvious from a much later Englishman, A. Courtney Williams, that it really wasn't cricket (a quite unintentional pun, I assure you) to fish imitations of the grasshopper. That may have been the prevailing view in the south of England, where artificials would certainly have been "looked on as lures rather than flies and as such . . . never made much appeal to English fly-fishermen", but no such distaste inhibited anglers elsewhere. As Courtney Williams observed, artificials were far more popular in America and Canada and on the Continent, though a particular one, he said, was popular among grayling anglers in Worcestershire, Shropshire, and Derbyshire. He didn't feel very happy about it, and neither did Francis Francis, who asked why it should be called a grasshopper any more than a gooseberry, which it much more resembled. You made it by wrapping lead around a hook, winding chiefly green wool ribbed with yellow or red or both, over the lead; and finished up with what looks like to us in the late 1980s as a round-headed ice-cream cone in miniature. You pitched this 'thing', as Francis called it, into every likely place, particularly in every deep eddy and swirly hole and worked it up and down, sinking and drawing with constant short jerks of the wrist. Grayling in some rivers just couldn't resist it, and yet in others it was ignored. In any case, Halford would not have approved.

Artificials much more imitative of the insect have since appeared (but still Halford wouldn't have approved), notably in the United States, and those of us in New Zealand and England who occasionally fish grasshopper patterns when the time is right assuredly profit from the excellent American dressings.

We can also draw on an astounding 28 grasshopper and 3 leafhopper patterns from 10 different countries described in Fadg Griffiths' sometimes rather odd book *The Lure of Fly-tying*. As well as the unanimity of six of the 10 countries on the best material to simulate grasshopper legs (they all use golden-pheasant tippets, and others use the same material for wings and tails), the strange thing about this Australian book with its understandable accent on the importance of grasshoppers is the complete absence of deer-hair grasshopper patterns. Body-materials range from golden pheasant to floss silk, tinsel to seal's fur, ostrich herl to chenille, with chenille by far the most popular. Although deer-hair had been embodied in flies for a good many years before *The Lure of Fly-tying* was published in 1978, Australians apparently had no use for it, and neither did they have a use for any of the innovative American grasshopper patterns embodying it, if Griffiths' list of adopted American patterns is anything to go by.

William Bayard Sturgis said as long ago as 1940 that for many years Michigan fishermen had used a pattern called the Michigan Grasshopper, but that it had a serious drawback. Although it was fished dry it was tied after the manner of a wet fly with an orange chenille body. While it floated for a short time if well oiled, it invariably rested on its side. Some tiers later dressed more satisfactory floating patterns, but in Sturgis' view nothing could compare with the hair grasshopper that appeared on the market around 1937.

Since then, a lot of grasshoppers have flowed under the bridge, some good, some bad, and some indifferent. But the best ones have come out of the States, and probably the best of the bunch is the Letort Hopper. With colour adjustments, it will double for grasshoppers anywhere, certainly in Australia and New Zealand, and no doubt in England too (though English flyfishers may choose to stay with Taff Price's modern deer-hair-bodied Green Grasshopper or Richard Walker's modern fine-grain-polythene-foam-bodied Grasshopper).

Clearly, an imitation is likely to succeed on any breezy day throughout the summer. Like the cicada, the grasshopper burgeons on hot sunny days. It grows in size as the summer progresses, so a range of sizes between 16 and 10 is recommended. Watch a real grasshopper on the water. It makes a disturbance trying to hop out of the clutches of the meniscus. You can simulate that struggling by twitching the artificial. Use nylon yarn or yarn fibres for body dubbing because the colour doesn't change when wet, or, if you favour clipped deer-hair bodies, colour them with an indelible felt pen. Learn to pitch the artificial heavily on the water as you would a cicada, and so plan or clip the dressing that it will sit flush in the film, not perched up like an imago of one of the stream flies proper.

Guard against the possibility of the grasshopper sinking by working silicone paste into the deer hair.

No doubt the original dressing of the Letort Hopper, developed apparently by Ernest Schwiebert and christened by Ross Trimmer on the Letort Spring Run River, has since undergone a few changes, but the basic ingredients and style remain the same. Vary the colours to match those of the naturals where you fish.

Hook: 16-10
Silk: Yellow
Body: Yellow yarn fibre
Head: Flared deer hair clipped to shape
Wing: Mottled turkey wing sections varnished and tied penthouse style along body
Hackle: Deer hair collar. Trim off any hair projecting below the body level.

GRASSHOPPER

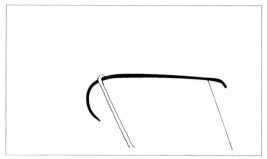

Tie in body yarn at bend and take thread to eye.

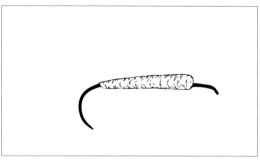

Wind to form tapered body.

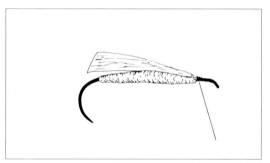

Tie in wing penthouse style along body.

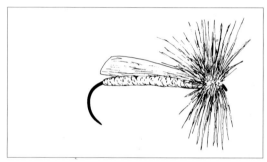

Spin deer hair to form collar.

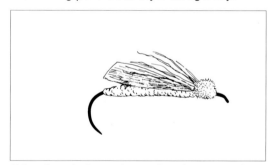

Trim deer hair to shape, leaving some long strands to brush back. Cut level with body under shank.

2
THE MUDDLER
IS THE GREATEST

Captain Hamilton needed only five flies in New Zealand to catch all the trout he wanted. They were all wet flies, and three of them were winged, and the captain fished them all with resounding success long before certain pooh-poohing pundits dismissed the logic and thus the likelihood of any winged natural fly ever being found below the surface. Those trout of the very early 1900s around Dannevirke apparently didn't know they were not meant to eat underwater flies with wings on.

Few anglers share Captain Hamilton's enviable confidence in just five artificials, whether his or anyone else's, but it seems that some pretty famous overseas flyfishers of the present day would be happy to plump for one basic pattern — provided they could make it a Muddler Minnow.

Their fly-boxes wouldn't necessarily exhibit row on row of identical Muddlers. A selection of sizes and colour-combinations and mutations would be there, but no-one would be left in any doubt that they all grew upon one Muddler family tree.

Dave Whitlock gives the fly his usual careful attention in Art Flick's *Master Fly-tying Guide*, 1972, saying, at the start of his section on the pattern, that no western fly selection could be considered complete without including the Muddler.

John Goddard terms it an exceptionally killing fly under practically any conditions, even where minnows are entirely absent. Charles K. Fox has called the Muddler the best-known minnow type of fly on the eastern slopes of the Great Divide. And if Richard Talleur were allowed only one pattern he would choose a Muddler Minnow. Why particularly? Because, he says, it is the greatest all-round fly in existence.

Perhaps no other fly represents so wide a range of trout foods. Ernest Schwiebert says, in *Nymphs*, that the ubiquitous Muddler Minnow fished slow

16

and deep along the bottom has taken many fish feeding not on sculpins but on dragonfly nymphs.

It is also taken for an emerger, a pupa, a nymph, a grasshopper, a minnow, a sculpin, a chub, a mouse, a caddis, a crayfish, a small trout, a stonefly.

As Whitlock goes on to say: "Given a wide range of sizes and several fishing methods it comes extremely close to being the only western fly you need."

Perhaps the appeal of this extraordinarily successful pattern is best demonstrated by the different depths at which anglers find it works wonders. One man, David J. Collyer, suggests that when lake fishing you will fish it most effectively just a few inches off the bottom. Work it with long, slow, steady pulls, pausing between each pull. Time the length of the drop until you connect with your first fish, for despite Collyer's belief that the most rewarding place is just off the bottom, you really do have to establish at what depth the fish are feeding at the time.

By contrast, in breezy midsummer weather especially, Bob Church finds that a Muddler skipped along the surface will bring stillwater rainbows to the attack. Fish it on a floating shooting head and strip it back fast. The big chop brought by a strong wind calls for a size 6 lure. Conversely, the gentle ripple in a light breeze requires nothing larger than a size 10. On bright summer days when fish lie deep he fishes a white version, and when fish occasionally fail to respond to the standard pattern he rekindles interest with an orange one.

By contrast again, Goddard finds the Muddler most killing fished just under the surface on a slow-sinking or sink-tip line and retrieved at a medium to slow pace. So there.

The Muddler's gift for impersonation at all levels and speeds has endeared it to New Zealand anglers too. We possess all the food items that trout apparently take the lure for overseas, so why shouldn't our trout respond in the same way?

And they do. Perhaps 1965 was not the inaugural year of the Muddler's appearance here, but in his book *Fisherman's Paradise*, Budge Hintz talks about the pattern, and the year 1965, and their coming together in Taupo, with great enthusiasm. Two American friends of his, Pete and Marg DuBois, brought Muddlers with them and proceeded to use the strange devices with telling effect.

According to Goddard, the pattern first surfaced in the United States in the early 1960s and didn't arrive in England until the latter half of the 1967 season. New Zealand has thus enjoyed a full two years more of Muddlers than England.

One of the most impressive instances of the pattern's virtuosity had enraptured a little man I met one day on the Major Jones Pool of the Tongariro. He was going to fish the pool for the very first time in 25 years of Tongariro experience, and he was going to do so with a Muddler Minnow. He told me that in desperation one day on an upper river pool, where nothing would come to any

fly he offered, he tied on a funny fly an American had given him. He fished the pool down with it once more, and took nine fish.

That day on the Major Jones I was only half-way up the bank on my way to fish the mouth of the Waimarino when the little man shouted. His maiden voyage down the pool with the funny American fly had already accounted for one rainbow. Half an hour later, fishing the wide mouth of the Waimarino with one of the Muddler Minnows the little man had tied up that morning and kindly given me, I too landed a rainbow, a 5lb jack rainbow this one, after a rather alarming battle to decide who should keep my precious Muddler, him or me.

When the little man and I had talked together he told me that his American benefactor had given him a Muddler Minnow correctly tied. The American must have examined some flies of New Zealand manufacture, for he told the little man that we tie it wrongly. I wonder, now, whether the American came from Don Gapen country in the States, Minnesota, for we know that Gapen invented the Muddler; but we also know that when the pattern reached Dan Bailey in Montana, that distinguished tackle-shop proprietor and fly-tier wrought some structural changes, "to suit western conditions", as Whitlock puts it.

Charles K. Fox may say that Dan Bailey was largely responsible for the Muddler Minnow's claim to fame, but it's well that Don Gapen's name is going to be remembered too. Between them anyway, two versions of a pattern have evolved which will catch trout consistently anywhere. Not that Don Gapen himself was the originator of the one Muddler feature that distinguishes the pattern: a bulbous head made from clipped deer hair had been embodied in certain artificials for years. Writing in 1940, for instance, William Bayard Sturgis said that the idea of hair bodies could have been brought to Chicago around 1912 by Emerson Hough himself, who stated that he had first seen flies tied that way on a fishing trip in the far north.

Ontario may just have been the place where hair-bodied flies originated. It was the home of the Algoma fly (tied with deer hair body and wings) and later of the Muddler itself. Don Gapen, of the Gapen Fly Co. of Anoka, Minnesota (although he has also been described as Don Gapin of Orillia, Ontario) set himself the task of imitating the flat-headed cockatush or cockatouse minnow, usually referred to as a muddler, or darter, common in northern Ontario's Nipigon river. His success is now legend, but whether the brook trout of the region for which Gapen is said to have tied the pattern fall for it any more enthusiastically than trout elsewhere I wouldn't really know, but I doubt it.

With all due respect for Don Gapen I'm impressed by Whitlock's enthusiasm for the Dan Bailey version, which he prefers to the original, but with due respect to Whitlock's specification I favour the Bailey dressing given by Budge Hintz in his *Fisherman's Paradise*. Through Pete DuBois, Hintz received a detailed dressing and instructions from Dan Bailey himself.

Construction is difficult. Goddard suggests that only the experienced fly-tier should attempt it. Talleur finds that of all the flies he ties and uses regularly, the Muddler gives him the most trouble. Correct proportioning; use of *fine* deer body hair; fashioning the collar and head on the *bare* shank; utmost care in trimming the head to shape — those are just four points to be observed in the making of this most challenging pattern.

Ringing the changes in colour and size will broaden the Muddler's repertoire of impersonations. Whitlock suggests experimenting with olive, black, white, browns, and golden yellow for the head-and-wing combination. And Talleur's best-ever Battenhill brown fell to a diminutive size 10 Muddler greased and fished as a grasshopper on the surface. Big Muddlers are not necessarily beautiful Muddlers.

Hook: 4,6 and 6XLS
Silk: Brown
Tail: Brown mottled turkey tied in like a short wing just before the bend of the hook
Body: Flat gold tinsel tied in first about two-thirds of the way to the eye of the

hook, wound down to the tail and evenly back to the starting point and firmly secured

Streamer: Small bunch of reddish brown calf hair, with a smaller bunch of white calf hair on top, tied in at head of body

Wing: Brown mottled turkey tied in at head of body as for standard wet fly

Hackle: Small bunch of fine deer hair tied in below wing and under shank of hook, with ends reaching as far as hook point

Head: Successive bunches of deer body hair spun with the tying silk round naked shank of hook from wing to eye. Five or six bunches of hair may have to be applied. The deer hair is then close-clipped to form a ruff head of short fibres right to the eye of the hook.

MUDDLER MINNOW

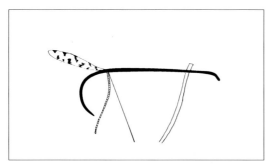

Tie in flat gold tinsel about one third of the length of the hook away from the eye. Take tying silk to bend and tie in small, mottled turkey feather for tail just before bend of hook.

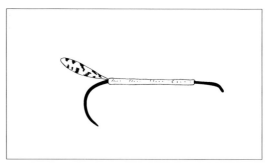

Tie in body, taking tinsel down to tail and back again.

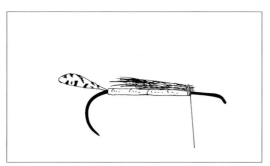

Tie in streamer, taking care to keep it on top of hook.

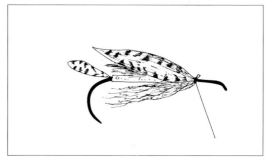

Tie in wing as for a standard wet fly and a small bunch of deer hair below body so that it reaches the point of the hook.

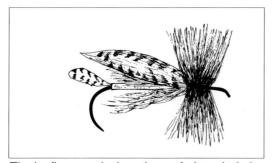

Tie in five or six bunches of deer hair by spinning around the shank of the hook, keeping the deer hair as dense as possible.

The deer hair is clipped (leaving some as a loose collar) to form a ruff head to the eye of the hook.

3
EVERGREEN
GREENWELL'S

Let us be thankful for the fastidious Tweed trout at Sprouston one day of May, 1854. They sent a Durham clergyman home from the river defeated. At least we must assume he was defeated: why else would he have taken back with him some specimens of a fly he could not remember ever to have noticed on the river before — a species to which the fish were rising, completely ignoring natural March brown flies on all sides — so that the well known Sprouston fly-tier James Wright could fashion an imitation?

Next day, armed with a dozen examples of the new fly James had tied up for him, Canon William Greenwell went to the river and had as fine a day's sport as he ever remembered. He filled his creel — not to mention his pockets too — with well over 30lb of trout.

Ever since Mr Greenwell's wonderful day of fishing on the Tweed, the Greenwell's Glory has accounted for millions of trout in many countries. It has become a favourite pattern, tied wet or dry, or as a nymph, or, more recently, as a spider, or as the foundation for a number of variations.

And yet, despite the examples of the natural fly on which James Wright modelled his imitation, and despite the clergyman's recollected conclusion, on capturing the naturals, that "the best imitation would be the inside of a blackbird's wing, with a body of red and black hackle, tied with yellow silk," no-one is certain exactly what the trout take it for. When olives are up, however, especially the large dark olive of spring, the artificial is freely taken.

Ernest Schwiebert, never one to be intimidated by orthodoxy, knew very well what two dozen rainbow and brown trout took his size 14 Greenwell's for one day on the Brodheads. It wasn't taken for an olive at all, but for one of the many caddis flies Schwiebert had watched climbing down underwater to lay their eggs. He fished the Greenwell's well downstream, retrieving it slowly along the bottom, and caught fish after fish. Maybe those trout could be excused for not knowing the difference between a mayfly and a caddis: Schwiebert's Greenwell's Glory was a down-winged olive version tied with whisks and woodcock wings, an entirely different animal from the Canon's.

When I first carried out some research into the origins of the Greenwell's Glory, in the mid-1970s, the earliest published authoritative reference I could find to the dressing was in William Henderson's book *My Life as an Angler*, printed in 1879. It's ten years later now, and I haven't yet found an earlier authority. True, Francis Francis' *A Book on Angling,* first published in 1867, does give a dressing, but one which is at odds with the original. Mind you, what I believe to be the first authoritative mention of the new pattern — authoritative because of Henderson's friendship with both Greenwell and Wright — was hardly over-described.

If no other book printed before 1879 carries the correct dressing, it means that the new and successful Greenwell's Glory trout-fly of 1854 wasn't revealed to the angling public for 25 years. But even in 1879, Henderson's specification was inadequate for any troutfisher anxious to tie the killing pattern for himself. He wrote of that historic time that "during the month of May, Mr William Greenwell and James Wright made some memorable days' fishing on Reddon Haugh. Morning after morning they were to be seen wading deep in the wide quiet dub above the stream called Brose. Happily for them each morning a breeze blew from the east, ruffling the surface of the water, and so causing their flies to hang leisurely over the fish. This circumstance, aided by lines cast 'far off and fine', enabled them every evening to show bumper creels, the remembrance of which still lingers in the neighbourhood of Sprouston. The work was chiefly done with flies dressed of feathers taken from the blackbird's wing, the bodies being formed of coch y bonddu hackles. So deadly did these flies prove that they have been awarded the commemorative title of 'Greenwell's Glory'. In spring and early summer I invariably use one on my cast of flies, and with the exception of the March Brown I have found none more successful". Notice that the 1879 revelation made no mention of a yellow silk body.

So, to imitate Canon Greenwell's presumed large dark olive, one needed in 1854 merely wings of feathers taken from the blackbird's wing, and bodies of coch y bonddu hackles. This at once suggests a kind of spider, admittedly a winged one, fashioned with a short body consisting solely of coch y bonddu hackle. Plainly, there's a world of difference between a spider and a fly, and one would suppose that an example of the Ephemeroptera should be dressed as a fly — certainly not as a spider.

However, such a supposition was utterly lost on a man who, in the late 1970s, a century after Henderson's book appeared, wrote a really sumptuous book on fly-tying and fly patterns, but put the record strangely awry for the

Greenwell's Glory by insisting in words and illustrations that the pattern should be dressed fully palmered, that is, that a coch y bonddu hackle should be wound palmer-wise down the length of the body. And yet he claims for his version that "the original and most popular dressing of the Greenwell's Glory".

Now, we know that fly patterns rarely remain absolutely true to the original, even if the original is elaborately detailed at the outset. So it was inevitable that the Greenwell's should be dressed as all kinds of 'look-alikes' while authentic details remained lacking. Even when they did emerge later on, as already instanced, the pattern appeared (and continues to appear) in many guises, and if James Wright of Sprouston were alive today he would be tearing his hair at some of the current caricatures, especially those marketed commercially, which still purport after 133 years to faithfully mirror the original.

The full and correct dressing of the Greenwell's Glory may have become common knowledge within a few years of the fly's debut in May 1854, but it seems most unlikely. Admittedly, Francis Francis came close to it in 1867, but it seems that although publication of Henderson's angling memoirs in 1879 stimulated immediate interest in the pattern, an accurate specification wasn't forthcoming until Canon Greenwell himself was persuaded to give it.

One such description was embodied in a letter dated June 1, 1900, which later came into the possession of A. Courtney Williams, the author of that definitive work on trout, sea-trout, and grayling flies, *A Dictionary of Trout Flies.* From the date of the letter, one can only assume that even at that late stage, 46 years after the pattern was first tied, the dressing was by no means well known — perhaps known to no more than a few friends of Greenwell, Wright and Henderson.

The letter assures the reader that the dressing is "the original and best edition of Greenwell's Glory". And it was:

Wing: Inside of a blackbird's wing
Body: Yellow silk
Hackle: Coch y bonddu
Hook: 14

And that's all that was said. What about the angle at which the wings were tied? Whisks? Was it floss silk or tying-silk? What precise shade of yellow must be selected? What about a ribbing?

It goes without saying that the pattern would be tied sparse, as befitted a fly from the north of the country, but as for the other characteristics and ingredients which are now taken as gospel, well, there would appear to be no authority for them. Tradition now has it, however, that the wings should be tied upright rather than sloped back in the customary wet-fly manner; that because the pattern did indeed imitate a wet fly no whisks were required; that a primrose-yellow tying silk should be used, *waxed with cobbler's wax to give an olive-yellow shade;* and that, as Mr Greenwell himself wrote in his letter of June, 1, 1900, "Gold thread can be added if wished" — although, at least from 1903, when E.M. Tod enthused over the pattern and wrote of ribbing with very fine gold wire, tiers have used wire in preference to thread.

So, if you seek a time-and-trout-honoured dressing of the large dark olive of spring, look no further than the Greenwell's Glory tied according to accepted practice and pattern. And thank your lucky stars that a Durham cleric way back in 1854, the year British and French forces landed in Crimea to fight their war against Russia, found Sprouston fish quite unresponsive to March Browns.

Consult Eric Taverner in *Trout Fishing From All Angles,* published in 1950, for instructions on tying the pattern, and exult with the author over his experience with the Greenwell's on a Highland loch: "In the straits between the islands we came upon the only sign we witnessed all that day of a rise to the natural fly. Upon the waters of a sheltered bay a fleet of large olives rode in perfect security, until a brace of trout discovered them and before any other fish should get wind of their good luck set about the work of polishing them (off) with such enthusiasm that one of them included in its collection a large Greenwell's Glory I had made haste to put on the water, the way a trout might notice it."

Courtney Williams notes that in Scotland anglers sometimes add a yellow tag to the standard Greenwell's, and in New Zealand a bright red tag. The Southern Hemisphere embellishment was entirely unknown to Keith Draper, New Zealand's authority on the trout flies of the region, when he published his *Trout Flies in New Zealand* in 1971.

Certainly the Greenwell's Glory has enjoyed an enviable reputation in New Zealand ever since it was introduced from England in the 1870s, but hardly the reputation imputed to it by the country's well-respected editor of the *Fishing and Shooting Gazette,* Mr F.E. Thornton, in the latter half of 1950. Admitting that he knew of no fly in New Zealand which the Greenwell's could represent, he also said, presumably tongue in cheek, that New Zealanders rarely used any other fly, so why worry . . .

Hook: 14
Silk: Yellow
Body: Yellow silk waxed with cobbler's wax
Wings: Inside of a blackbird's wing
Hackle: Coch y bonddu.

GREENWELL'S GLORY

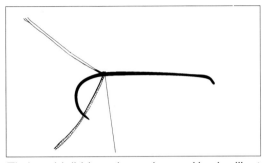

Tie in gold ribbing wire and waxed body silk at bend.

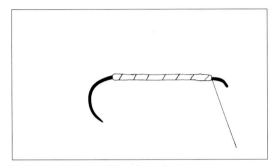

Take body to position for wing.

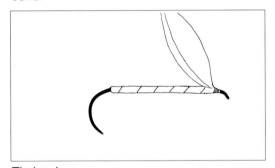

Tie in wing.

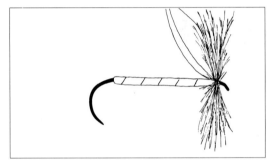

Tie in hackle and finish in normal way.

4
WOOLLY WORMS
ARE WONDERFUL

Some trout-fishing regulations are absurd. Perhaps, years and years ago, angling or poaching practices dictated certain provisions which nowadays are no longer relevant. Nevertheless, outmoded or ineffectual regulations persist, year after year, and one wonders why. Possibly it's because change, even change supposedly for the better, is not always welcome, and because a consensus among sportsmen and fishery managers may be reached too late each year for law-draughtsmen and licence-printers to amend and print new-season's licences on time. And then, between seasons, opinions change, or resolution weakens, and then it's too late, again.

Two absurd Taupo trout-fishing regulations keep on keeping on. You can be sure that more than two skulk in the thickets of legal jargon and small print confronting the honest angler, but only two concern me right now.

First, I just have to mention the Glo-Bug. This obnoxious lure, which imitates a trout-egg or cluster of trout-eggs, was introduced to the Tongariro in 1984 by someone who quite plainly thought that catching trout is the be-all and end-all of trout-fishing. Suddenly, because of the ease with which running fish could be taken on imitation trout-eggs, every shameless man and his dog descended on the Tongariro, and chaos began to reign.

Sundry punch-ups enlivened the contemplative man's recreation. Possession became nine-tenths of the law on the river, especially the possession of immovable entrenchment in a pool. Fishing manners and angling values went to pot.

Subsequently, someone embroidered the Glo-Bug frenzy with lead weight and bead-chain eyes. One or two so-called flyfishers even introduced ground-baiting, as it is called by coarse-fishers in England; scattering food down a rapid and then fishing the pool below. In this case the food was genuine trout-eggs. The

Glo-Bug sent down after the ground-bait did great execution. That was a blatant breach of the regulations. In fact, it was two breaches.

In my view, the regulations were broken when the Glo-Bug was first introduced and used. No matter that the fishery-authority, after months of subsequent acrimonious discussion between anglers, came out in favour of the lure: one had only to ask fishermen what Glo-Bugs imitated to be told, by nine out of ten, "trout eggs".

And, of course, the regulations say that no person shall use any fish roe or any imitation of fish roe. So nine out of ten anglers using Glo-Bugs would knowingly have been using imitation trout-eggs. They are still doing so. No prosecutions have taken place.

Which prepares the ground for my second absurd Taupo fishing regulation. It governs another prohibited lure, whether natural or artificial: the creeper. Fly-tiers may use or imitate all sorts of natural insects but they are forbidden to use or imitate the creeper.

For those who don't know, our New Zealand creeper, *Archichauliodes diversus*, is the larval form of the only aquatic member of the insect order Megaloptera in the country. Sometimes known as the toe-biter, or black fellow, or black creeper, the larva has cousins all around the world, including North America, where similar insects are known as hellgrammites. We call the adult, winged, insects Dobsonflies, or lace-wings, or alder flies. In Britain they call them large stoneflies, for there it's the stonefly larva which is known as the creeper.

This largest of our stream insects has long been known for its strong appeal to trout. Years ago, G.E. Mannering found that if he fished it well upstream away from the mouths of the rivers, the creeper was the most deadly bait that could be used. No doubt it still is. The large larva makes as delicious a mouthful now as it did a century ago. Ever since men began to fish for browns and then for rainbows here, they have known that the natural creeper has been the thing to use as bait if you want to catch fish from a river. I remember a Wellington friend who often fished the Hutt River at Maoribank gleefully telling me one Monday morning that though he had been able to find only five creepers along the riverside the day before, each of them had accounted for a good Hutt brown trout. Writing in 1892, W.H. Spackman said in *Trout in New Zealand*, that the creeper was the finest possible lure for trout:

"Use a hook about No.6 in size and pass it through the little square black head, letting the grub hang down its full length. About 2 or 3 small shot, or, better still, 2in. or 3in. of fine lead wire wrapped round the gut, should be placed 8 in. or 10in. from the hook. Throw, if possible, upstream into all the little eddies."

Twelve years later, the colourful Captain G.D. Hamilton, author of *Trout-fishing and Sport in Maoriland*, let us into the secrets of the ideal creeper-container:

"This should be a japanned zinc flask, 8in. high, $2^{1}/4$in. across the bottom, 1in. across the top, with a strong hinge lid, round in shape, perforated over its whole height, and it should have a zinc handle $^{3}/4$in. in diameter and $^{3}/4$in. wide and fastened $1^{1}/2$in. from the top edge of the flask. It should be hung from a button-hole by putting twine loop round the flask and through the handle."

Bill Crawford and I could have filled a couple of the Captain's creeper-flasks one late-summer morning along the Waipunga in the days before God and the Forest Service made a mess of the river. The water was pleasantly low, but less generous than usual, giving up only four small fish and four bigger ones. The largest was a jack rainbow of a little under 2 kilograms which scooped up my *Aoteapsyche colonica* imitation in the bypass below the Concrete Pool. His stomach was packed solid with a moist green pâté in which millipedes, green beetles, and net-building caddis were embedded like cherries in a fruit-cake. Oddly, though, I didn't find a single creeper in the pâté, and yet every other streamside stone seemed to shelter one of the succulent larvae. We unearthed dozens, ranging in size from two to five centimetres. We found pale brown stonefly nymphs too, and dark brown *Coloburiscus humeralis* nymphs, but that day belonged to the creeper, and I shall always remember it that way. Most probably the absence of creepers in the stomach of my rainbow was accounted for by the concentration of the insects at the edge of the stream. The larvae migrate out of the water to pupate under stones, and we were there at that time of year.

No doubt we could have fished the natural on No.10 hooks, tippets judiciously weighted with lead shot or wire, and got away with it; but even in the knowledge that one may legally fish other natural insects in the Taupo fishery, but doesn't, who would want to break the law and fish a forbidden creeper? But why not an imitation?

Sure, in days gone by, live-creeper fishing conjured trout out of rivers as readily as magicians conjure rabbits out of hats. George Ferris called the larva a deadly live-bait for very large trout in deep holes. Captain Hamilton fished his deadly creepers on two hooks between size 12 and 8, Dublin limericks, both fastened on one piece of gut so that the point of one hook lay about $^{1}/2$in. from the point of the other, and I've no doubt that where the natural insect and two hooks are legal, it is fished that way still.

Perhaps it is not so surprising that New Zealand artificials were a long time developing. Live creepers were easily found in the summer under stones along the riverside, either just in the water or just out, so where live insects were permitted and worked so well, why bother with tying imitations?

Both Norman Marsh, in his *Trout Stream Insects of New Zealand* and Keith Draper, in his *Trout Flies in New Zealand,* draw attention to the scarcity of New Zealand artificials.

While no good purpose is served by tying imitations of the winged insect, which apparently only flies at night (although I once watched one flying clumsily down the Tauranga-Taupo River in broad daylight), there's every reason to fashion and fish likenesses of the larva — unless one fishes at Taupo, of course.

One can understand the reason for banning the natural, but banning the artificial is ridiculous. If authority refuses to recognise the Glo-Bug as an imitation trout-egg, however, it can hardly be expected to associate an artificial creeper with the real thing, can it now? And if you are ever questioned about an artificial which looks suspiciously like a creeper, you can always say it is a drowned caterpillar look-alike, just as the odd Glo-Bug user may say that his imitation trout-egg is only pretending to be a harmless cotoneaster berry.

Keith Draper appears to have been the first to publish a New Zealand dressing for the creeper. I haven't been able to find one in his definitive *Trout Flies in New Zealand*, but in his later booklet, *Nymphs For All Seasons*, published in 1973, he describes a pattern he calls the Weighted Woolly Nymph, which "serves well if fished along deep rocky runs, especially in streams where creepers abound". Tony Orman gives Jim Ring's dressing in his *Trout With Nymph*, and Norman Marsh details a dressing in *Trout Stream Insects of New Zealand* .

I prefer Draper's pattern, even though it is not explicitly a creeper imitation.

Ring's peacock-herl body and separate black hackles tied at intervals along the body, and Marsh's peacock-herl body and turkey-herl thorax, don't appeal to me as much as Draper's brown chenille body and palmered hackle. He doesn't give the hackle colour, but I assume it's the same as the colour used in the dressing of the Woolly Worm lure described in his book *Trout Flies in New Zealand;* that is, grizzly.

All in all, however, I favour an American dressing, the one Charles Brooks gives in his *Nymph Fishing For Larger Trout.* Again, it's not explicitly a creeper or hellgrammite imitation; it can be passed off as an underwater stage of a stonefly, a dragonfly, an American riffle-beetle larva, or a damselfly, as well as a hellgrammite. Brooks recommends hooks ranging from 4s to 10s. He's serious about 4s — in the States hellgrammites "at maturity will be three inches long and thick as your little finger". One of the smaller species sounds very like ours, and even answers to virtually the same name, *Chauliodes.*

Like Draper, Brooks calls the pattern a Wooly Worm (not a Woolly Worm, though), and his dressing is:

Hook: 4-10
Silk: To match body
Tail: None
Body: Chenille, of proper size and colour to suit
Hackle: Grizzly is first and original choice, but brown, black, ginger and badger are all used. Weight as desired.

He recommends black thread; tying the head large; using five and not seven turns of hackle the length of the body; and using no ribbing.

WOOLLY WORM

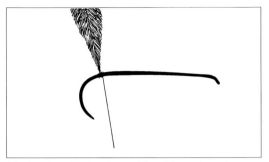

Tie in chenille body and hackle at bend.

Tie body to eye.

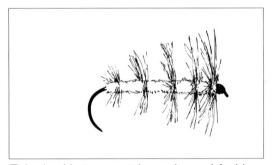

Take hackle to eye, tying palmered fashion.
Tie off and make head with tying thread.

5
CHIRP AND SLURP

Summer trout are suckers for cicadas. No other terrestrial provokes such excitement in fish or, for that matter, in fishermen. When the wind flings those big winged insects on river or lake, trout rush for them and wolf them down, and flyfishers thank their lucky stars that, for once, they've no need to lay an imitation feather-light upon the surface.

Moreover, cicadas burgeon throughout those brilliant breezy days when just to be out by river or lake is joy enough. Often hours of exploration and stalking lie ahead, while sun-worshipping cicadas chirrup and chirp continuously, and summer-fat trout wait to take them with a satisfying slurp from the surface.

Even Mottram of the chalkstreams, 75 years ago and more, when most troutfishers here were still impaling live cicadas on their baithooks and casting them like artificials, even Mottram spoke of the importance of beetles, grasshoppers, and 'cyads' in Tasmania and New Zealand, foods he felt which called for the serious attention of the dry-fly fisherman.

Picture him now in your mind's eye, tired after his three-quarter-mile hip-high wade through Reece's Lake, but suddenly invigorated by his first view of the creek that flowed out of it. Reece's Creek, so like the Kennet of England, held at least half a dozen trout of from 3lb to 6lb which he could see from where he stood, and every so often one would rise slowly up and with what he described as a "luscious suck" take something from the surface. A strong wind was blowing, and he suspected that the fish were taking cicadas. They were. "Very soon with a cyad fly," he wrote, "I was in the heat of mighty battles."

Summer cicada fishing can indeed bring on mighty battles, or at least the promise of them. One Boxing Day on the Waipunga, just before we needed to return to the station wagons and meet our third member for our ritual white wine and Christmas-leftovers lunch, Brian Morgan and I prepared to join battle with

the brown trout that customarily lies alongside the toitoi bush on one of the last pools of a morning stalk. He was there. We both saw him. But by that time the heat of the morning decided us to relax for a few minutes behind a big screen of toitoi, Brian to tie on a buzzy green Cicada and I to shed the fishing vest and extract the flask for a measure of sweet black tea each.

Pouring tea, I smiled at thoughts of cicadas and flasks of 80 years ago and more. Around Dannevirke at least, and if you were Captain Hamilton himself, the flask you carried in cicada-time was a cicada flask, of japanned zinc, and perforated throughout, from which you extracted a cicada from time to time and caught a trout from time to time.

Some minutes later Brian inserted himself into the toitoi on our side and began lengthening a cast well away from the fish before switching it across to the toitoi reflections over the stream. At the crucial moment, a gust of wind drove the line back and slapped the Cicada on the surface three metres from the trout, which rushed it like a tiger. Brian almost overbalanced in surprise, cursing, and struck too soon. The fish flounced back to cover. And that was that, apart from snorts of laughter all the way back to the wagons for lunch.

While cicadas are about, trout throw caution to the winds. Clumsy casts won't put them down provided you don't line them. Back-country rivers and streams with plenty of bankside or overhanging vegetation always seem the most likely cicada waters, but if the day is bright and breezy, and cicadas are chirping endlessly away upwind of bigger rivers and lakes, there's every chance of furious activity every now and again on those waters too as the occasional wind-blown cicada crash-lands on the surface.

A good cicada year is one of the events the summer Tongariro flyfisher looks forward to. And as for Lake Otamangakau, well, it only takes a windy summer's day at the height of the cicada presence to banish any thoughts that perhaps the lake is getting fished out.

Stung by report after report of big trout falling suicidally for cicada patterns a couple of summers ago, I drove down myself to catch a limit. En route, the weather changed. I arrived to a still, grey, day. My lone green Cicada lay upon the surface the only one for miles around, and yet two fish upped and ate it. I lost them both.

That year, Cicada patterns evolved at Otamangakau almost daily. The cicada carnival wasn't restricted to the Big O of course, though I guess that for pure concentrated feeding and fishing effort the lake would have been hard to match. Latterly, as artificials became more and more sophisticated around the shores of the lake, you could always tell whether a flyfisher was using a plastic-winged pattern. It whirred backwards and forwards like a bee with a hangover.

Mottram fashioned his imitations with hare-fur bodies cut to shape, brown silk heads, and white cock-hackle wings. He did not allow for legs because "they cannot be seen when the fly is viewed from below."

Clipped deer-hair or shaped polystyrene bodies coloured green or brown with a felt pen make more satisfactory bodies these days, and furthermore they usually float for as long as you want them to. Study the natural cicada closely before tying imitative patterns: the body shape and the way the wings fold are important to copy closely. On the other hand, impressionistic Cicadas catch fish too, the Mole Fly for instance, tied exactly like a palmer but with a green or brown silk body to match the cicada of the moment, and wings of mottled hen pheasant.

Although the natural has no tail in the sense that mayflies have tails, Norman Marsh obviously finds that a tail doesn't detract from the impression his dressing makes on the trout. He ties in the deer-hair tail first, spins a series of deer-hair collars tightly from tail to thorax, and then trims them to make a plump body. He ties in the wings next, and then fastens hackle and peacock herl, wrapping the herl to form a thick collar, then winding on the hackle, then taking the thread forward to make a big head.

The ingredients are:

Hook: 8-12
Silk: Brown
Collar: Peacock herl
Body: Deer hair
Hackle: Brown cock
Wings: Badger hackle tips
Tail: Deer hair.

CICADA

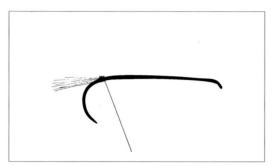

Tie in tail of deer hair, leaving hook bare.

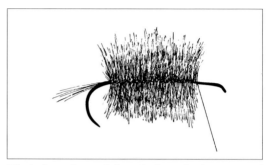

Tie in bunches of deer hair, spinning around hook.

Trim body to shape. Tie in wings.

Tie in peacock herl and hackle.

Wind on and finish in normal way.

6
THEODORE'S QUILL

At least two of the 750 copies printed of Sir Herbert Maxwell's big book *Fishing at Home and Abroad*, published in 1913, sit solidly on Taupo bookselves. One of them belonged for many years to Greg Kelly, who first made known to us in New Zealand something of the origins of the Kakahi Queen.

Enshrined in that large and luscious volume of Sir Herbert's is a contemporary account of trout fishing in America written by a man called Theodore Gordon. That chapter was the closest Gordon ever came, in his lifetime, to publication in book-length form. This "Father of dry-fly fishing in America", this man whose own trout-fly invention, the Quill Gordon, had by 1912 already enjoyed six years — or was it nine? — of fame along Catskills rivers and beyond, never published anything more substantial than his contribution to the book for which Sir Herbert had sought an American chapter.

True, he did embark on a full-length book at some stage. By 1915 it was sadly only about half-finished; sadly firstly because he died on May 1 that same year, and sadly secondly because relatives burnt the manuscript, supposing, in their ignorance, that it harboured the deadly tuberculosis bacteria which had killed Gordon.

Starting in 1890 in the English magazine *Fishing Gazette*, however, and then in 1903 in the old American magazine *Forest and Stream*, Gordon regularly contributed angling and natural history notes and observations. And he kept up a prodigious correspondence with local and overseas troutfishers, including Halford and Skues. Much of Gordon's writing was rescued from oblivion by John McDonald in 1947 when, after years of effort and research, that angling historian and scholar published *The Complete Fly Fisherman; the Notes and Letters of Theodore Gordon*.

Like Greg Kelly, Gordon knew no Latin for his stream insects apart from such family names as Ephemeroptera and Plecoptera. He only knew dozens of stream-flies of his day by their looks. But looks were quite enough. He carried details of all of them with ease, locked away in his mind.

This slim small flyfisher of the Catskills who died in 1915 at the age of 60, has become a legend. Not only in the United States, but also everywhere else where trout are to be found in running waters, his name survives in the dry-fly pattern he developed to imitate the duns of the first substantial spring mayfly of the Catskills season.

Try to imagine this frail little man just before the start of the new season on Neversink or Beaverkill. Here he is, towards the end of winter, immured in his house, longing for spring. He is writing an item for *Forest and Stream* magazine. It appeared on April 28, 1906.

"It is a bitter cold winter's night and I am far away from the cheerful lights of town or city. The north wind is shrieking and tearing at this lonely house like some evil demon, wishful to carry it away bodily or shatter it completely. The icy breath of this demon penetrates through every chink and crevice, of which there appear to be many, and the wood-burning stove is my only companion.
It is on nights such as these, after the turn of the year, that my thoughts stray away from the present to other scenes and very different seasons. We return in spirit to the time of leaf and blossom, when birds were singing merrily and trout were rising in the pools . . ."

By the time that article of his was published, trout may have been rising in the pools of the Neversink to the first of the large mayflies of the Eastern spring. And what more natural than that Theodore Gordon, released at long last from the grip of winter into the awakening riverside world once more, should hail the familiar stream flies of the season and set about offering delicate imitations of them to the hungry trout?

Some angling scholars say that 1906 was indeed about the year in which Gordon perfected the pattern which was to help make him a legendary figure among American flyfishers.

Later that same year, on August 11, the English *Fishing Gazette* referred to the pattern for the first time. Remember Gordon had been writing for the magazine on and off for 13 years, but no mention of the Quill Gordon pattern, as such, had been made before that date. However, just as Leonard M. Wright was convinced in 1972 that Gordon "had quite another fly in mind" than the one his pattern was supposed to imitate, so I question the year ascribed to the birth of the Quill Gordon.

When you know that Gordon first became seriously addicted to the dry fly early in 1900 after he had received some examples of the great F.M. Halford's flies direct from the master; and when you know that he was already an innovative fly-tier, and had already devoted much of his life to flyfishing, six years seems a long time for a pattern to be evolving. No-one seems to know when the dressing was definitely decided and the Quill Gordon finally launched, but if something Gordon wrote in 1912 describes the fly for which posterity continues to salute him, then 1903, not 1906, is much closer to the year of the fly's debut. He writes in his 1912 account of American trout fishing in *Fishing at Home and Abroad*:

"I have killed a great many of the best fish on a fly that has been very troublesome, as the quills and hackles are rare over here. In England they would probably be easy enough and we can have three shades of dun, dark, medium and light, in quills and hackles. This gives a number of flies that are often plentiful in spring and early summer. The wings are plain wood duck, split, a light feather, giving the effect of semi-transparency, not dull and heavy, as are many of the wings used. This fly has been in use nine years so has proved itself."

In articles and correspondence about the Quill Gordon, its designer repeatedly drew attention to the "very troublesome" nature of the fly, by which he meant the difficulty of procuring both peacock quill and hackle of the correct shades and quality.

Although he does not mention the fly by name in the above passage the qualification "very troublesome" leaves little doubt that he was writing of the Quill Gordon.

His mention of a plain wood duck wing, split, does cast a little doubt on the theory, since Gordon was an advocate of rolled and not split wings for the duns he imitated; but if he was indeed talking of the Quill Gordon he may still, in 1903, have been following a particular English technique, not yet having developed a preference for the rolled wing.

On the other hand, he implies that he dresses the pattern in three shades, dark, medium, and light — a range of options mentioned in places elsewhere as being most desirable for Quill Gordons, in order to imitate the different shades of the male and female flies and the seasonal changes of the species. On occasions, Gordon veered off the straightforward communications track, assuming you would follow without difficulty. If only he had named a name, or given the dressing detail rather than leave his reader to interpret that particular 1912 message correctly, we could be closer to the actual year of the Quill Gordon's debut.

It was not at all surprising that Gordon knew nothing of the scientific names of the flies he found along the river: no books of American anglers' flies were published in his lifetime. Jennings' *A Book of Trout flies* was the first authoritative work to appear — 20 years after Gordon's death.

Halford's *Floating Flies and How to Dress Them*, published in 1886, introduced Gordon to the dry flies of England, but it is generally thought that he taught himself fly-tying from a copy of a book by another Englishman, Alfred Ronalds, whose classic, *The Fly-Fisher's Entomology*, had first appeared in 1836.

R.B. Marston, the highly respected editor of the English *Fishing Gazette*, was able to say of the American's standard of fly-tying in 1906: "Mr. Gordon makes a handsome trout fly. I should think few, if any, American anglers know so much about our flies and fly making and dry-fly fishing as he does. He sends me a fly on an eyed hook dressed by himself, called the 'Quill Gordon', quill body, silver-grey hackle, with a bunch of summer duck fibres for wings — it would kill anywhere."

You can understand why Gordon chose to imitate the first important mayfly of the new season. Emerging from his own annual winter hibernation, eager to steep himself in the wonderful reality he had only been able to dream about for so many weeks, Gordon felt compelled to indulge his hunting instincts as quickly and as fully as possible. You can imagine him practically falling over himself in his need to enjoy fishing pleasures again. And even for Gordon, that early advocate of fishing for sport and not for meat, fishing pleasures nevertheless meant deceiving, hooking, and landing trout.

In the beginning, full of admiration for Halford and the exact-imitation school, Gordon studied the early mayflies very closely and sought to copy their colours and shapes precisely. Years later, he knew that exact imitation was not a mandatory ingredient of success and he recognised that his Quill Gordon could be taken for several different naturals. Writing to Guy Jenkins on March 5, 1912, for instance, Gordon said that as a fly it was typical of certain ephemera. And later that year, in a letter to Skues, he admitted using the artificial in three shades. If body and legs hit off the natural, he said, the fact that perhaps the wings were the wrong colour did not seem to count against the fly.

Although no exact identity was hinted at in any of Gordon's published notes and letters as collected by John McDonald, Jennings believed in 1935 that *Iron (Epeorus) pleuralis Banks* was the mayfly Gordon's fly imitated.

Known nowadays simply as *Epeorus pleuralis* (which covers for *Iron (Epeorus) pleuralis, E. fraudator*, and *E. confuscum*) the fly is admirably represented by the Quill Gordon (or Gordon Quill as some call it) on Eastern streams. On Western waters, a dark Quill Gordon on size 14 hook serves equally well to imitate the male dun of the *pleuralis* equivalent in the West, *E. longimanus*, and an ordinary Quill Gordon on size 12 hook for the female.

Most obligingly, at least in the East, *Epeorus pleuralis* is a creature

conveniently set in its ways. You could describe it as a rather conservative insect except that in fast water its duns insist on freeing themselves from their nymph cases on the bed of the river instead of at the surface. Apart from that unmayfly-like idiosyncracy, *E. pleuralis* toes the line most helpfully. When the water reaches 50°F (10°C) you can expect the fly to hatch. Two to three days of such comparative warmth will ensure good hatches. Once begun, the regime won't falter, even though the temperature may drop 15° overnight. Hatching conveniently takes place at around the same time each day, between 1pm and 2pm, but the season doesn't normally last longer than about a month, say from the third week in April to the third week in May in Eastern streams (and usually a month later in Western waters).

Many stream insects of the same species differ slightly in colour from location to location. The natural Quill Gordon appears to be no exception. Greyish bodies, black and white underbodies, and cream-coloured 'bellies' faintly olive in hue have been met with. Usually, though, the body displays pronounced alternating bands of light and dark, and these are faithfully represented by a piece of stripped quill taken from a peacock's shoulder feather. Smoky-blue wings, two long tails, and legs showing distinct brown marks, complete the description of *E. pleuralis,* except that the female is larger and lighter-coloured than the male.

As Jennings wisely remarked: "As this is one of the most important flies in the fly-fisher's book of flies, it is recommended that both the male and female be represented . . ."

Gordon's own tie for his fly was:
Body: A strip of bi-coloured peacock quill ribbed with fine gold wire
Tail: 3 or 4 fibres from a wood-duck feather
Hackle: Smoke grey
Wings: The unbarred feather of a summer duck
Hook: 12-14.

In one way Gordon's "very troublesome" fly has become far less so; peacock quill is easily obtainable (although the essential two-tone quills can still only be obtained from about one in 20-25 of the feathers from eye portions of the peacock shoulder plume).

But the summer or wood duck is a strictly protected bird now. When that plumage is unobtainable the fly-tier uses dyed mallard or mandarin flank feathers. Edmund Burke, writing in 1931, however, gave it as his opinion that mallard was never as satisfactory as summer duck.

Tying techniques vary from tier to tier. It would be nice to know how Gordon proceeded but he was most protective of his fly-tying secrets and left us no written record of his methods. Standard procedures, given in scores of fly-tying books, are easily applied. If you have access to Richard W. Talleur's *Mastering the Art of Fly-Tying,* however, you just can't put a finger wrong: here are 14 pages of directions on tying the Quill Gordon, illustrated step-by-step by no fewer than 62 photographs. Whether you dress the pattern according to Talleur, or Burke, or Jorgensen, or Schwiebert, or Overfield, or Morton, or any one of a dozen others, it's the most wonderful fly that ever was. Knowing that, and using a Quill Gordon, and following the precept Gordon is almost as famous for, "cast your fly with confidence", you really can't go wrong when *Epeorus pleuralis* is up and about.

Hook: 12-14
Silk: Tan or pale yellow
Tail: 3 or 4 fibres from a summer duck feather
Body: Strip of bi-coloured peacock quill
Ribbing: Fine gold wire
Wings: The unbarred feather of a summer duck
Hackle: Smoke grey.

QUILL GORDON

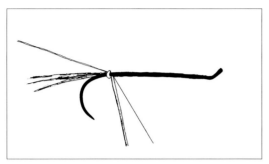

Tie in tail, peacock quill and ribbing wire.

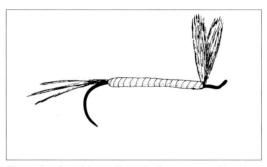

Form body with quill and rib to eye with wire. Tie in wings.

Tie in hackle so that it flairs around wings and finish off.

7
DAINTY
DAMSEL

If you stand in the water or on the bank at Lake Otamangakau on a hot summer's day, when hopefully the nagging wind so many of us know so well there has diminished to almost nothing, for once, you will become aware of dainty damselflies dancing in dozens over the water. Throw a floating line out and 20 of them, ruby-eyed, will settle on it before you can begin a retrieve.

I have yet to pull one through the tip-ring, but they do tend to cling to the line until the very last moment. In the days when I used to rely on an indicator to signal the take of a trout at the nymph, I had the occasional fish come hot-fin to the indicator. But so far I have never had a fish come gallumphing to any damselfly riding daintily on the floating line at Otamangakau.

And such a lack of enthusiasm for the winged damselfly on the part of rainbow and brown trout at the Big O, and at most other places too, is well known. It's true that emerger patterns are tied and used now and again but, just as perhaps one will never have need of a winged dragonfly imitation, so one likewise fails to think in terms of a dry damselfly.

But the nymph is an entirely different kettle of fish. Nymphs of both the dragonfly and damselfly are taken avidly by trout wherever they are found. Polly Rosborough observed, many years ago now, that nymphs of the damselflies are far more important in the trout's food chain than most of us realise. On slow-moving streams and reed-bordered lakes and ponds, he said, the population of damselfly nymphs is almost unbelievable.

You would believe it at Lake Otamangakau especially, though maybe not so readily were you fishing deeper lakes without a generous growth of weed. Standing in McGivern's Bay on summer days at Otamangakau, I have so often looked down and found a little wriggling damselfly nymph manfully striking out for something solid to climb up, to help its metamorphosis into winged existence; but only once or twice in Lake Taupo have I encountered them,

Certainly there will be Taupo bays in which damselflies proliferate in the kind of numbers Polly Rosborough talks about, but not in the bay that I so often fish. Strangely, however, that particular bay once drew an enthusiastic local entomologist to its shores time and again, throughout the summers of his younger days in Taupo, to further his studies into the dragonflies which were so common there. Dr J.S. Armstrong specialised in the Odonata of the region, and told me that, judged by the unbelievable numbers of the nymphal shucks of dragonflies he found there, sometimes well up the trunks of the willows, a hopeful angler could do far worse than tie up and fish imitations there at the proper time of year.

Obviously, the entomologists know pretty well what they're doing, but I find it a little difficult to accept their classification of damselflies with dragonflies. Odonata is the order, and the order is spoken of as the order of dragonflies. Even so, true dragonflies occupy just one of two Odonata suborders, the Anisoptera. Damselflies belong to the other suborder, Zygoptera. I suppose the combined suborders take the name dragonflies because there are more of them than damselflies and they're bigger. Certainly this is so in New Zealand, where only three damselfly species have been identified as against the ten of the dragonflies, according to the Entomological Society of New Zealand's Bulletin No. 5, *Guide to the Aquatic Insects of New Zealand*, by Michael J. Winterbourn and Katharine L.D. Gregson, published in 1981.

The differences between the two suborders are considerable, and although it's more than obvious that some likenesses characterise the suborders too, it's the differences that, to me, pull them widely apart. Even the old name for the damselfly that I remember from my earliest days of fishing and reading about fishing, the demoiselle, or maiden fly, evokes nothing of that fierce and terrible summer predator the dragonfly. The demoiselle, damosel, or damselfly should surely never be mentioned in the same breath as that deadly airborne interceptor? Behold the dragonfly arrowing past, changing direction so fast to snap up an insect that your eye loses track. Then watch the gentle damselfly flutter across the water: does it, too, catch and eat insects in flight?

But we are concerned with an earlier existence, a wandering existence in search of prey among the weeds and detritus of lake-beds, and sometimes the beds of backwaters and slow sections of rivers too. Here, damselfly and dragonfly are equally energetic predators, the one slim and elegant, the other bulky and clumsy. Each hunts with an extremely efficient articulated grab poised for action under the lower jaw. Called a mask, this grab shoots out like lightning once the victim is in range. So although one's so fat and one's so slim, these differing members of the Odonata do have an articulated grab in common. Maybe that's the one characteristic which brought the old-time entomologists to lumping dragonflies and damselflies together.

Quite apart from size — dragonflies are, on the whole, much larger than damselflies — and shape, they each hold their wings quite differently when at rest. The dragonfly's are always at right angles to the body, the damselfly's folded together along the back.

But the one feature that to me would have to debar a damselfly from a dragonfly club is its breathing apparatus. Like the nymphs of the mayfly, for instance, the nymphs of the damselfly breathe with leaf-like appendages called gills. Mayfly-nymph gills are usually arranged along the sides of the body. Damselfly-nymph gills, however, look exactly like a fairly substantial three-pronged tail which extends about half as long again as the abdomen.

Across the way, that dumpy, laboriously-clambering member of the Anisoptera sports no such posterior decoration. He breathes through his bottom. True. And some can so regulate the speed of 'exhalation' as to jet-propel themselves out of trouble in little spurts when need be. True again.

So you see, articulated grabs aside, these two Odonata suborders haven't a great deal in common. But the trout don't mind. One thing trout themselves have in common is unqualified approval of the Odonata, however much the members of the two suborders may differ.

Helpfully for anglers and fly-tiers, the larvae, or nymphs, of the three damselfly species may be readily imitated by dressing bodies in only green or brown or a mixture of both. But, you will ask, what particular shades of green or brown? And I will refer you to the waters in which you wish to hook trout on damselfly imitations. Catch some nymphs. Note colours and sizes at different times and different places. Even note the colours of the bed of the lake or river at the points chosen. J.G. Pendergrast and D.R. Cowley, in their *An Introduction to the New Zealand Freshwater Insects*, 1966, weren't just idly gossiping when they said of the red damselfly *Xanthocnemis zealandica* that "Larvae can to some extent regulate their colour to conform to the background; the colours are limited to greens and browns". Which, if the authors had been addressing anglers, is another way of saying "match your artificials to the naturals where you fish"; and that advice is always invaluable, whatever the natural you wish to imitate.

Bear in mind that the damselfly is at its most vulnerable when on the way to hatch. It wriggles up from the bottom in search of a weedstem or rock poking out of the water. That wriggle is significant. As John Goddard pointed out in 1977, in his book *The Super Flies of Still Water*, "over the years, most still water fly fishermen have realised that one of the most difficult forms of underwater life to imitate is this wriggling action of the damosel nymph as it swims along". Schwiebert and Whitlock in the States, and Goddard in England, have advocated hinged-body patterns, but, hinged ot not, any pattern needs to be dressed on hooks with extra-long shanks. Tie a slender body tapered from head to tail.

Emphasise the segmentation of the body and the gills at the posterior end.

When you fish it, you may choose one of a variety of successful retrieval options. Starting with Rosborough, who advocated one-inch very fast jerks of the tod-tip and line, you can work right through to the other extreme as recommended by Brian Clarke: "long slow draws of 2ft at a time . . ."

Patterns for damselfly artificials evolved relatively recently, and most of them have originated in the United States. The Bowlkers, in their *Art of Angling*, published in England almost two and a half centuries ago, emphasised that the dragonfly was used only for salmon-fishing. They didn't mention damselflies. A. Courtney Williams, in his definitive *A Dictionary of Trout Flies* first published in England in 1949, gave it as his opinion that although nymphs of the Odonata are liked by trout, the larger ones were too big and solid to copy with any degree of success.

Some of the modern American patterns, notably those of Schwiebert, Whitlock, and Charles Brooks, have become deservedly well known, and so have those of C.F. Walker and Goddard and Clarke in England.

In New Zealand, damselfly patterns have been slow in coming forward, chiefly because of the influence and excellence of overseas patterns. Nevertheless, Keith Draper, Tony Orman, and Norman Marsh have published patterns.

Orman lists a damselfly dressing, not his own, among the patterns given in his book *The Sport in Fishing*, and it's that one I want to reproduce here.

It's a dressing from Bruno Kemball, whose small tackle shop and fly-tying establishment with the Red Spinner name across the front stood for so many years alongside the main highway at Hatepe, between Taupo and Turangi. A bristly military English moustache, and a sense of humour enlivened by a picturesque vocabulary, made conversations with Bruno thoroughly memorable occasions. Furthermore, he and his wife tied some of the finest trout flies you ever saw. Bruno died in 1985, the year that claimed Budge Hintz and Mike Pattison and Greg Kelly too, here in Taupo.

All Bruno's patterns and Bruno's ways of tying flies died with him except, as far as I know, for a few dressings in Fadg Griffiths' book *The Lure of Fly Tying*, and the dressing of a damselfly nymph which he gave to Tony Orman.

Here it is, partly because it's a thoroughly good pattern, and partly because too few tributes were ever paid to "the last of the pukkha sahibs".

Hook: 6 or 8, preferably long-shanked
Silk: Olive
Tail: Bunch of partridge grey breast feather, dyed olive green, 6mm long, tied down slightly round the bend of the hook
Body: Tie in at tail gold wire or fine oval tinsel and a 'sausage' of mid-green wool. Taper body to two-thirds of shank and secure
Ribbing: Tie in one strand of herl from the proximal end of a peacock eye feather and bring down in eight equal turns to tail. Secure with two turns of tinsel, which is brought back to head, eight turns in the opposite direction, to overlay or lay alongside and protect the herl
Thorax: Two close turns of brown chenille
Hackle: One partridge brown plumage feather, tied in by the tip, two turns brought down and finished off as a splayed throat hackle to represent the legs.

DAMSELFLY NYMPH

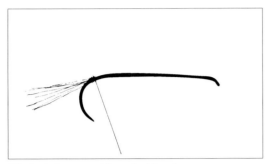

Tie in tail around bend of hook

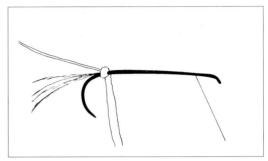

Tie in gold wire or tinsel and sausage of green wool. Take thread to eye.

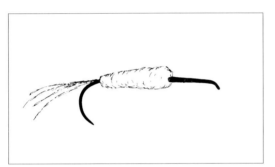

Taper body to two-thirds of hook length.

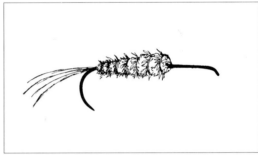

Tie in peacock herl and rib in eight turns to tail. Secure with two turns of wire or tinsel then rib it back to end of body overlaying herl with wire to protect and secure it.

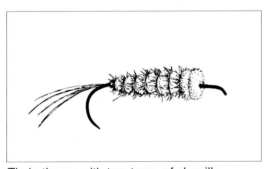

Tie in thorax with two turns of chenille.

Tie in hackle by tip then finish off as splayed throat hackle to represent legs.

8
SUPA-DUPA-PUPA

Earlier this week, at eight o'clock of a mild spring Taupo night, moths and midges, but chiefly midges (chironomids) seethed at our windows. We're 30 metres or so above the lake, and it was the first mild still night since snow fell unseasonably along the ranges a few days ago. After a lazy day of sunshine and fluffy cloud, insects were out in force.

The next night was even calmer. Chironomids swarmed at the lighted windows. They had been heralded by a lone male which arrived before dusk and clung to the glass as though reserving a place for later. His body was about 4mm long. The magnifying-glass revealed him as an astonishingly handsome insect, with dark plume-like antennae, a dull red thorax, a distinctly segmented body emerald-green for three-quarters of its length and dull red for the rest, long dull-red forelegs, emerald-green middle and hind legs down to the 'knees' and dull red after that, and pale grey wings folded down flat along the top of the body.

Later on that evening, studying scores of the winged insects, I was struck by the overwhelming predominance of males, all of which appeared to have read David Collyer's recommended body material for the English Grey Midge Pupa pattern, stripped peacock herl.

Midges are those non-biting but mosquito-like gnats that hatch from most standing areas of water large and small. They also hatch from rivers and streams, especially slow-moving ones. They live in silt or mud as thin wormlike larvae up to 20mm long which at times twist and turn their way up to the surface.

The largest and most common New Zealand species is *Chironomus zealandicus*, more familiar, in its larval form, as the bloodworm, because of its normally rich red colour. Other species have larvae which are yellow, brown, green, virtually colourless, purple, or pink.

The bloodworm, which is common to countries all over the world, is a most unusual insect in that its haemoglobin content, which gives it its colour, allows it to thrive in oxygen-deficient places, notably in the muds of deep lakes. For instance, in Lake Taupo, where the larvae apparently comprise a quarter of the fauna, *C. zealandicus* lives happily in larval form at depths of more than 100 metres.

Few anglers fish imitations of the bloodworm — and certainly don't do so at 100 metres — but I know one man, a Lake Otamangakau specialist, who has taken a great many trophy rainbows and browns there on a thin, red, braided-silk, detached-body pattern. I was there, fishless, myself one day, when he appeared from nowhere and proceeded to hook, land, and return his tenth fish of the morning on his tiny bloodworm imitation fished alongside one of the big weedbeds just south of McGivern's Bay. That was the place, incidentally, where on a later occasion I took my own largest rainbow, a fish of 4.5kg, on a brown and red chironomid-larva imitation.

Although larval imitations are not unknown, it is normally conceded that while the inert bloodworm is easy enough to copy, the twisting and turning swimming action so characteristic of the insect is impossible to duplicate. Despite the success of the Otamangakau specialist's pattern, then, it really is more rewarding to fish imitations of the second underwater stage, the pupa. Even so, that innovative angler and fly-tier Dr J.C. Mottram, whom I draw to your attention on other pages too, designed patterns imitative of both larva and pupa as they hang down from the surface film. Mottram bound tiny wedge-shaped pieces of cork to the shanks of very light hooks, inked them black, and, in the case of the pupa, added two or three grey barbs from an emu's feather to either side of the head (to represent the normally-white breathing 'plumes'), and cast them to rising fish. Charles Brooks improved on Mottram by using tiny polypropylene pieces, instead of cork, inside small sections of nylon stocking. Goddard and Clarke improved on Brooks by replacing polypropylene with pieces of a more efficient floating medium, the closed-cell plastic foam marketed as Ethafoam, also enclosed in pieces of nylon stocking.

Such attention to fly-tying detail underlines the importance of the midge pupa to trout and troutfishers, especially at first and last light. Never mind that pupae may be ascending in scores, or hundreds, or thousands. And never mind that some of the experts offer contradictory advice, some dismissing ultra-realistic patterns as unnecessary and some insisting that plumes, for instance, must be copied; some exclaiming over the brilliant crimson body of the New Zealand bloodworm and some calling it dull red; some advocating any number of different-coloured bodies for artificials, others recommending chiefly black ones. The midge pupa is a truly essential pattern for stillwaters and some running waters.

Let's examine this humble little insect more closely. Brian Clarke, who startled the fly-fishing world with his admirable book *The Pursuit of Stillwater Trout*, says very emphatically that trout eat pupae in immense numbers, and in fact that stillwater trout eat more midge pupae than anything else. Clarke's opinion is not necessarily true of Lake Taupo, for instance, where trout are believed to dine principally on smelt and bullies, but on smaller and shallower lakes he's no doubt right (and he may well be right for certain shallow and weedy areas even of Taupo).

Schwiebert writes that the midge's role in flyfishing has been "somewhat unnoticed". Whitlock agrees. Marsh points out that the insect is probably the most prolific food available; further, that artificials can be fished throughout the season.

Writing of Taupo's chironomids, Dr D.J. Forsyth said in *Lake Taupo*, 1983, that the average population density of *C. zealandicus* larvae in 1974-5 was 187 per square metre; that the species favours the deepest waters; that larvae moult four times, over-wintering as fourth-stage larvae; that between 100 and 1,000 eggs are laid in a gelatinous envelope; that several generations occur each year; and that fourth-stage larvae moult to reveal the pupa which, within about 48 hours, leaves its larval tube on the bottom and rises to the surface to hatch.

Hudson found as long ago as 1892 that about a day before the pupa heads for the surface it assumes a silvery appearance owing to the release of air between the body and the pupal skin. Further, Harris found much later that when chironomid pupae are hatching at the surface the tail end of the shuck fills with gas, immediately assuming a greatly enhanced lustre, as of a glass tube filled with mercury. He believed the phenomenon explained the added attraction which a flat tag of gold or silver gives to many artificial flies.

Anglers have long observed that, as in the case of larvae at the surface, trout take pupae slowly and deliberately; that the pupa is the most common cause of both morning and afternoon rises; that suitable artificials will kill throughout the season; that the pupa exhibits an extremely bulky thorax, which occupies one-third to one-half of the length of the insect; that the winged insects will sometimes clump together on the surface in golf-ball-sized crowds; that stillwater larvae are most active at twilight and in darkness.

Fly-tiers should note that because of its proportionately large thorax and curved shape, the pupa looks rather like a comma with a long tail. Dress it that way, accentuating the bulk of the chesty thorax and tapering the body down to the tail, which should be taken round the bend of the hook. Bodies should be distinctly segmented. Realism can be enhanced by tying in small white tufts at head and tail. One way to do this very neatly is to tie in a length of suitable white wool or yarn on top of the shank, leaving an end poking out fore and aft. Trim the ends into short tufts when the imitation is complete.

That idea comes from Dave Hughes, author of the 1987 book *Handbook of Hatches*. Like his writing, Hughes' patterns are simple and straightforward. He ties his midge pupae with fur bodies though, and I must say I prefer the crisper outline of silk or yarn, both of which may be bought in many colours of course, thus avoiding the dyeing chore.

And talking of colours, pupae, generally speaking, hatch into winged insects of the same basic body-colour. The pupal thorax is often darker than the abdomen. There's only one way to settle on the colours you need for your waters, and that is to catch yourself some winged adults and preferably pupae too. Failing that knowledge, a selection of pupal imitations with bodies of bright red, dull red, chestnut, grey, emerald-green, pale green, and black, will cater to the collective taste of most trout. But such a solution to the colour problem does mean tying and carrying a lot of midge pupae.

I guess most pupal patterns are successful, but I haven't yet come across one which appeals in its entirety. Putting aside questions of colour, two versions are necessary, one fished below and one at the surface. The underwater one, which should be allowed to sink deeply and twitched very slowly to the surface, needs no built-in flotation material, but the floater at the surface does. Roger Fogg's dressing for the sinking version is admirable, as is David Collyer's for the floater,

but with two minor additions to both: distinct white tufts fore and aft (the aft one half the size of the other), and a tag of ribbing wire or tinsel at the tail. Collyer's deer-hair thorax is excellent provided you use hollow deer hair and build just enough weight into the abdomen to make the pattern float at the surface tail down.

One of the advantages of the deer-hair thorax, incidentally, is the ease with which it can be shaped to a true midge-pupa thorax profile, which bulges down rather than up.

Fogg's pattern is:
Hook: 10-16
Silk: To match body
Body: Floss silk. Rib darker colours with close turns of fine copper-coloured wire, lighter colours with fine silver wire
Thorax: Dub a fat seal's fur thorax about a third of the hook shank in length, in a colour matching that of the body.

Collyer's pattern is:
Hook: 12-16
Silk: To match body
Ribbing: Flat gold, silver, or copper Lurex
Body: Floss silk or feather fibre
Thorax: Deer body hair.

MIDGE PUPA

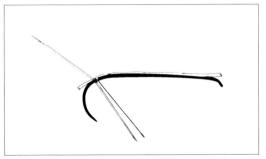

Lay wool for tail and breathing 'plumes' along hook. Tie in body silk at bend with wire.

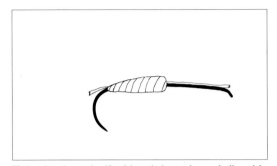

Take body to half of hook length and rib with wire. Tie on body material made by dubbing seal's fur on to thread.

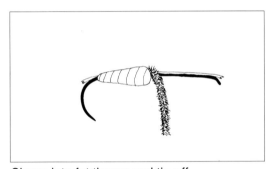

Shape into fat thorax and tie off.

Tease out tail and plumes.

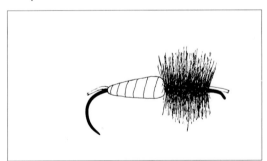

OR: If using deer hair for thorax, spin hair around hook shank and tie off.

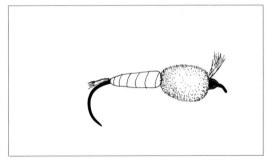

Trim to shape and tease out tail and plumes.

9
SAWYER'S
INTERNATIONAL NYMPH

Much to my sorrow, Mrs M. Sawyer's little nymphs have all gone. Too late I've realised that I ought to have put aside, for posterity, one of the 14 Pheasant Tail Nymphs she airmailed out to me in New Zealand in the late 1960s.

True, I can tie reasonably exact imitations of the original Sawyer's Pheasant Tail Nymph myself without difficulty from any one of a dozen fly-tying books. Still, I wish I had been sensible enough to keep just one genuine example straight from Frank Sawyer's wife: after all, by the late 1960s, the pattern had already achieved a remarkable reputation as a deceiver of trout. Over the intervening years it has lost nothing of its appeal for fish, fishermen, and fly-tiers, and now occupies an honoured place among the classic patterns. Oliver Kite, that other outstanding Avon flyfisher, called it "one of the most effective patterns ever devised by man". If it had earned that reputation from careful tying procedures aimed at ensuring that materials and weights and sizes and proportions were consistently observed, I am now without a single proven original on which to base future successes . . .

Frank Sawyer, the Wiltshire Avon river-keeper who designed the pattern, initially developed it of course for the Avon, but his Pheasant Tail Nymph takes trout wherever they are to be found. Intended to represent an English mayfly nymph belonging to the group of olives available to trout at midsummer and for the following few weeks, the pattern nevertheless finds acceptance wherever species of small brownish swimming mayfly nymphs are found.

That is one of the great strengths of the Pheasant Tail Nymph. Its appeal as an artificial imitative of a whole range of brownish nymph species has been abundantly demonstrated for years, which says much for the inventiveness of the man who designed it. Sawyer felt that for the average flyfisher exact imitation was too complicated a goal: if a single pattern representative of several different

but similar species could be developed, and proven in practice, then anglers would be well served.

Quite apart from its popularity with trout, the pattern pleases fly-tiers themselves immensely. Sawyer deliberately chose simple, inexpensive, and easily obtainable materials for all his popular nymph patterns. This one, the Pheasant Tail, embodies only two ingredients: herls from the ruddy-coloured central tail feathers of a cock pheasant, and the finest red copper wire.

Sawyer's studies of swimming nymph species in the Avon and of the eating habits of the river's brown trout, made several things very clear to him. Nymphs live most of their lives close to the bottom. Trout take the major portion of their food well below the surface. Swimming nymphs exhibit continuous movement: at rest their rows of gills or breathing appendages vibrate and when swimming they work much faster. The tail — not the legs — propels the insect along. The legs are, in fact, held close to the body during the action of swimming.

Such movements, or an appearance of movement, must be given to the artificial if it is to be successful. The flue of the pheasant feather herls ripples in a lifelike manner, and the fanned tail-whisks seem to pulse, once the current or the angler, or both, help work the nymph seductively in the water.

Obviously, if trout take most of their food well under the surface, the nymph must be worked at the level at which trout are accustomed to expect it. In most cases, then, it would need to be weighted. To simulate the rippling movements of the 'fringe' of gills on each side, fibres which will wave about are needed, and a quite distinct tail. No hackle, to represent legs, is necessary because the swimming nymph does not use its legs for propulsion.

My recollections of the genuine Sawyer nymphs are of tiny artificials. Compared with the size 10s and 8s for nymphs in common use for rainbows at Taupo, for instance, the 16s to 14s tied for the browns of the chalkstreams seemed minute. Mind you, those small nymphs are as much in demand in places in New Zealand as anywhere where browns are to be stalked, of whatever size, but the majority of the hooks on which the pattern is tied and fished here would be considerably larger than 16s. The copper wire would be of an appropriately heavier gauge, too.

I am a little reluctant to mention another memory of the elegant little Pheasant Tail Nymphs that came to me from Court Farm House in Netheravon: but I did find them of a rather delicate constitution. I can believe that they were quite robust enough to emerge virtually unscathed from encounters with the smaller brown trout of the chalkstreams. Faced with the brutal enthusiasm of much larger trout — and especially of Tongariro rainbows often weighing 5lb — they were inclined to go to pieces. Small wonder.

But the pattern was and is extremely successful here. That is the important thing. Having established its effectiveness, we only need to tailor its dressing to the needs of the water and the size of the natural. And I think, for those who care to preserve the original tie and at the same time benefit by its simplicity, it is appropriate to follow the directions of the master, Frank Sawyer, himself.

Bear in mind that the pattern was designed to solve the problem of getting a nymph to feeding trout lying deep. Trout close to the surface taking nymphs ascending to hatch were not the target. Hence the copper wire — the weight essential to take the nymph down.

That much older nymph fisherman, G.E.M. Skues, fished imitations of ascending nymphs to trout close to the surface. He perfected the technique that brought only disapprobation from the dry-fly bigots of his day and finally forced the old man off his beloved Itchen water.

Sawyer's studies and methods complemented those of the older man, but happily he was spared poor Skues' sorrow. The Avon reach on which Sawyer was employed as keeper for the Officers' Fishing Association saw a change in angling regulations in the late 1920s to permit the practice of upstream nymphing. Formerly, as on much chalkstream water, only the dry fly had been allowed.

One of the dry flies which would have regularly taken trout—and no doubt still does — from that reach of the Officers' Fishing Association's water, the stretch between Fyfield and Amesbury, is also known as a Pheasant Tail. According to A. Courtney Williams in his *A Dictionary of Trout Flies*, the pattern is "one of the greatest patterns for all-round fishing, and possibly the most useful all-purpose fly extant. Fished wet or dry it is an effective representation of a number of flies . . ."

Sawyer's nymph differs substantially from both the Pheasant Tail pattern attributed to the Devonshire angler Payne Collier, in 1901, and from the pattern devised by Skues and published in his *The Way of a Trout with a Fly*, 1921. Their patterns, by comparison with Sawyer's, are complex. Sawyer's is simplicity itself.

As far as is known in the history of fly-tying, no-one before Sawyer had advocated and used copper wire instead of tying silk, but that is what Sawyer did, in order to carry his nymphs down to the trout. So, all the fly-tier needs is a supply of pheasant-tail herls and a reel of the finest red copper wire. Sawyer himself specified wire that was very little thicker than a human hair. Speed and depth of water would govern the weight needed — or, rather, nymphs could be tied with varying amounts of wire to suit the depths at which they needed to be fished.

You build up the nymph shape with windings of wire, forming with them an abdomen sloping back to the tail, and a pronounced thorax. You select three or four strands of pheasant-tail herl and tie them in so that the tips form a fanned-out tail 3mm in length. Then you twist the herls round the wire and wind them almost to the eye. Separate the strands and secure them with a turn of wire. Wind the wire back to behind the thorax. Bring the herls together and take them back over the top of the thorax to form wing-cases and fasten them with one turn of wire at the base of the hump. Return the wire with a wide turn or two to the front of the thorax. Fold the herls forward over the top of the thorax, cut off the ends of the herls, and neatly cover the stubs with another couple of turns.

Ideally you should experiment with different lengths of herl until you can ensure that the invariably lighter-coloured tips of the herls form the body of the nymph and the invariably much darker butt ends form the wing cases.

Now, if you favour hooks somewhat larger than those Sawyer used, you will wonder where on earth you can buy cock pheasant tail feathers large enough to yield the long herls you'll need. You can't. What you must do is wind on successive sets of herls, preferably reserving the lighter portions of the strands for abdomens, and the darker portions for wing-cases.

Hook: 10-16
Silk: Finest red copper wire
Tail: 3mm-long tips of body fibres
Body: Four browny-red fibres of cock pheasant tail feather.

SAWYER'S PHEASANT TAIL

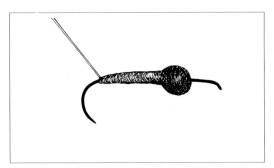

Winding with copper wire, form abdomen and thorax.

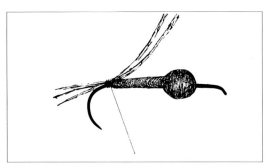

Tie in at tail 3 or 4 strands of pheasant tail herl.

Twisting herls with wire, wind around body to eye and secure.

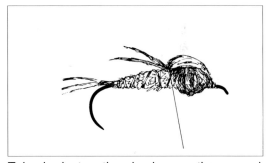

Take herls together back over thorax and secure with one turn of wire.

Take herls back to eye and secure with wire.

10
SALUTE
THE SMELT

We should build a monument to *Retropinna retropinna*. Like the roach of England (but not for the same reason), our humble little fish with the long Latin name deserves everlasting homage, accolades and acclaim. Well, around central North Island lakes anyway. Its introduction to certain South Island lakes has not been attended by the success achieved at Taupo, for instance, and this is a continuing sorrow. Anyone aware of the outstanding presence and influence exerted by the smelt in the lakes to which it has been successfully introduced does not need to be reminded of the huge debt we anglers owe to this silvery little relation of the Salmonidae.

Most obligingly, the sea-going population from which thousands of smelt were netted from the Waikato River at Mercer in 1907 for transfer to Lake Rotorua forbore to turn up their toes and die. In fact the fish thrived in their new, solely freshwater, environment. Other lakes holding trout showing signs of deterioration were accordingly stocked with smelt too. It's said that it only took two years for the poor quality trout in Lakes Tarawera and Okataina to show a marked improvement after smelt were introduced in 1932.

As a consequence of that experiment, smelt were turned into Lake Taupo to halt the deteriorating condition of trout there in the 1930s. Between 1934 and 1939 five consignments totalling more than a quarter of a million smelt were released into the lake. They brought salvation to the fishery.

Now, although it forms the major food of trout in the lake, and is consequently harried here there and everywhere, the smelt manages to hold its own very well indeed thank you, and unless some disease or other disaster decimates the population it will continue to keep the ever-hungry trout of the lake in good condition.

Of course, *Retropinna retropinna* must not be associated only with lakes. In fact, it is a species largely of the sea, although freshwater populations other than lake populations exist too. Where it can migrate between salt water and fresh it spends most of its life at sea, but moves into fresh water at two years of age to spawn. Shoals of two-year-olds enter most rivers from about mid-October onwards. No-one yet knows anything about their lives at sea, and no-one really understands why some of our big rivers, like the Waikato, Manawatu and Clutha, should swarm in spring with one-year-old smelt travelling upstream on incoming tides.

G.E. Mannering, that gifted all-round sportsman who wrote *Eighty Years in New Zealand*, believed that, of the two varieties of smelt in the country, one came in from the sea to spawn, and the other went up the rivers to mature, coming down again in autumn. He was grateful for such migrating smelt when he fished a Waiwakaiho river pool close to the sea in 1904 or thereabouts. A companion and he frequently fished the pool at night during that season and took about 50 browns, averaging 6lb, on smelt (*kaihuka*, the local Maori called them). The trout wouldn't normally take in daylight, but Mannering's largest fish, weighing 10 ½lb, did, and paid the penalty for its diurnal misdemeanour.

Estuarine brown trout particularly appreciate the migration of smelt from seawater to fresh. Similarly, the spring movement of lake smelt into tributary rivers and streams excites the interest of browns and rainbows. Late last spring I vividly remember a day well down the Tongariro, where hawthorns frothed white with blossom and the river ran slow under old willows and grassy banks, for all the world like a south-of-England coarse-fishing river in May. Every so often, though, big rainbows came questing along the banks for smelt edging up from the Delta. They made splashy lunges for the little fish along the weedy stretches, and if we peered into the gaps between the blackberry and scrub overhanging deep bends we could watch them hunting the smelt just below us.

They wouldn't touch anything we offered them. So often, trout will ignore just about every smelt imitation you throw at them. At other times, the first pattern you tremblingly tie on in the presence of wildly smelting fish will bring an immediate response. On an all-too-brief visit to the mouth of Lake Taupo's Whanganui River early in 1987 I put out a Grey Ghost in front of the crowd of rainbows working the rip, and it was taken second cast.

No other trout-fishing experience is quite as exciting as the occasion on which you find trout hunting smelt within casting distance. Usually it's a case of getting into action quickly before the hunters and the hunted move elsewhere; the faster you can find an acceptable pattern, the better you will be pleased!

At Taupo, at least, the smelting excitement begins with the appearance of shoals of two-year-old smelt, ready to spawn, in the shallows off beaches and stream mouths in spring.

While the smelt congregate over the clean sands they want for their eggs, trout will eat their fill, often appearing to herd the little fish together like dogs herding sheep.

For many years, our knowledge of the smelt in Lake Taupo was very sketchy indeed. Following the three-year study of the lake populations initiated by the Wildlife Service and carried out by Dr R.T.T. Stephens, the life cycle and habits of this major food of Taupo trout are now extremely well researched. Flyfishers throughout the country, and particularly those who fish at Taupo, should read what Dr Stephens says about the smelt in his contribution to the DSIR's book *Lake Taupo*, published in 1983.

He found, for instance, that in 1980 it was not uncommon to discover counts of 50,000 smelt eggs per square metre in stream sands. Off the beaches, though, the density of eggs rarely exceeded 5,000 per square metre. Eggs hatched into larvae, or alevins, 3-6mm long, in 8-10 days. At nightfall, 'enormous numbers' of alevins would emerge from stream-bed sands and drift into the lake.

Dr Stephens discovered things of absorbing interest to anglers: for instance, that whereas smelt favour the lake surface by night, they descend and gather near the thermocline, at 25m-35m, by day. And when you know, as revealed elsewhere in *Lake Taupo*, that zooplankton, the food of larval smelt and bullies, rise to the surface about two hours after sunset and descend again shortly before dawn, the smelt's own daily 'rise and fall' is easily explained, but is no less significant for flyfishers.

When the thermocline sinks deeper in autumn, the smelt go down with it, becoming less abundant at night at the surface. And during the winter they move into still deeper water, from 60m down, and are then few and far between at the surface after dark. When spring comes, the two-year-olds move into waters just below the littoral zone preparatory to spawning. Soon they will all be dead for, like the quinnat, none survive the traumas of spawning.

Imitating the smelt is relatively easy. Many have tried and many have succeeded. Patterns complicated and patterns simple have been developed wherever the use of the natural smelt became prohibited. Many Taupo lures are taken for *Retropinna retropinna*, whether or not they bear any resemblance to the little fish. After all, to a fast-moving rainbow on a smelting spree, there's surely no great difference between a rapidly retrieved Parsons' Glory or Mallard Smelt, or a rapidly retrieved Grey Ghost or Taupo Tiger? The smelt is one item of food which dashes for its life, especially at the surface, when danger threatens, hence the disturbances trout make when in hot pursuit.

So you would think, wouldn't you, that provided your retrieve is fast, any old slim bright pattern will do? But unless I'm unique in my frustration at pernickity smelting trout, I find it difficult to select the right pattern. Nevertheless, we can be quite sure that the great haste of escaping smelt is on our side: trout

just haven't got the time to give an imminent victim more than a fleeting glance. All the same, many other potential victims are probably careering around close at hand and unfortunately may look far more appetising than your offering.

For another thing, though, size rather than colour is all-important. I haven't given that factor enough thought in the past, but I have just looked out a small collection of flies tied, perhaps 50 years ago, at the start of the Lake Taupo smelting phenomenon, by that great flyfisher and famous lodge proprietor Alan Pye, and I am suitably impressed by an aspect of fly-tying which had gone to the back of my mind, inexcusably. True, the four smelt flies in the Pye collection look like black-headed blowfly maggots with long tails. They were tied with off-white wool or silk bodies ribbed with silver or dark thread, and with tails of fibres from a pale hawk's feather. The significant characteristic of all four, however, is the small hook on which they are tied: size 10.

As Draper wisely observes in his book *Angling in New Zealand*, the smaller and simpler your smelt fly the better it will kill. On the question of simplicity, he recalls the success of Tom Hope's smelt pattern, which the old Taupo angler called his Hope's Special. It was merely a white-bodied fly with a tail of a strand of sugarbag fibre. No wing, no hackle.

Some of our fly-patterns are beautiful to behold, virtual works of art which it seems a shame to get wet, let alone attacked by trout. I am all for carefully imitative dressings when necessary. Such occasions are usually dictated by the length of inspection time a trout can give an artificial, but in the case of the smelt, it would seem that simplicity an*d small size* are fundamental to success.

Hence the pattern I've decided on, Draper's String Fly, a version of Tom Hope's smelt imitation, but with one concession to extravagance; that if pieces of white string or sugarbag fibre are unobtainable, four or five long fibres from a pale hawk's feather may be substituted . . .

The dressing is:
Hook: 10
Body: White wool
Ribbing: Silver
Tail: White string or jute fibre from a sugarbag.

Footnote: I don't know whether Tom Hope of Taupo and D. Hope of Canterbury were related, but both became excellent flyfishers and both designed smelt-flies; the Hope's Special of Tom Hope and, among others of D. Hope, the well-known Canterbury lure Hope's Silvery (a 'silvery' being the name by which the smelt is known in some parts. It may still be known in places as the cucumber fish too, a name descriptive of the smell of the fish).

SMELT

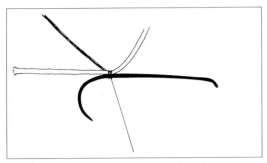

Tie in tail, wool and ribbing at bend.

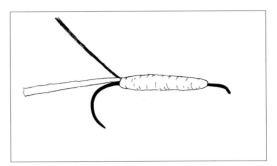

Wind wool to eye and tie off.

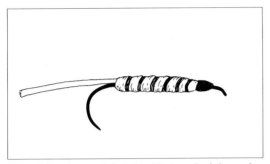

Rib with wire and finish with head of thread.

11
THAT WELSH
BEETLE

You can imagine the excitement of the would-be anglers of New Zealand when at long last the time came for them to fish for trout for the very first time.

Painstakingly introduced from England via Tasmania after years of frustration and failure, the brown trout had been the first to arrive safely, in 1867. Sixteen years later along came the rainbow from California. Within a few years of their arrival, trout and salmon tackle brought out from Britain by the early settlers was at last being put to use. Listen to what Mr R. Chisholm had to say about the very first occasion of all.

"The morning longed for by the disciples of Isaac Walton had arrived, and long before a streak of light broke across the horizon on the first day of December, 1874, the enthusiastic angler, with pulse beating fast and strong, could be seen with rod and line wending his way to the favourite stream. The Water of Leith, from its proximity to Dunedin, was the chief scene of operations, and our respected townsman Mr A.C. Begg, who had for many years taken the liveliest interest in acclimatisation, was the fortunate angler who had the distinguished honour and satisfaction of landing from the stream the first trout caught with rod and line in New Zealand waters."

We don't know what fly deceived that very first trout, but you can be pretty sure that the pattern originated in Britain, and it doesn't take a shrewd angler to surmise that it probably hailed from Scotland itself. In fact, if it wasn't one of Stewart's spiders, either black or red, I would be most disappointed: the Scots would have taken a special pride in honouring such an important event with national reminders appropriate to the occasion.

If not with a spider, Mr Begg may have taken his trout on a Coch y Bonddu. "Perish the thought!" any Scot might say, disdainfully, expressing a sentiment which in turn would ruffle the hackles of the Welsh. But never mind, the name

coch y bonddu certainly comes from Wales, but the beetle itself is apparently common in Scotland too. Furthermore, in 1874 the pattern was already well known as a first-class fly on all waters.

That early reputation has grown and grown with the passing years. The artificial is known and used throughout the world. And as Courtney Williams says: "Wet or dry and at any time of the season, it is always a good pattern to try on a strange river." Did Mr Begg know that, I wonder?

Like so many of the trout flies introduced into New Zealand, the Coch y Bonddu had already enjoyed a long history of success in Britain. In fact, according to John Goddard, who researched the fly's origins, references go back to the late seventeenth century (although he may have meant the late eighteenth century). True, the fly he assumed was the prototype, so to speak, of the Coch y Bonddu because the dressing was so similar, was the Welshman's Button, or Hazel Fly, described, he says, in *The Angler's Museum,* by Thomas Shirly, the second edition of which appeared in 1784.

As is so often the case with popular flies of long-proven appeal to trout and troutfishers, the little red and black beetle of Wales is known by several other names. As well as the Welshman's Button and Hazel Fly, the artificial is called at times the Fern Web, the Bracken Clock, the Marlow Buzz, the Shorn Fly, the June Bug. Trying to bring some order to another problem, the problem of identity, and so establish once and for all that the Welsh know a coch y bonddu beetle when they see one, and wouldn't confuse it with other beetles as some fishing writers were doing, Courtney Williams wrote to a number of anglers in Wales in 1931 or thereabouts. He asked them please to send him specimens of the insect known to them as the coch y bonddu. Without exception, he said, they sent him coch y bonddu beetles, known in the taxonomic world, incidentally, as *Phyllopertha horticola.*

One of the popular names for the beetle, the June bug, is not unexpected: the beetle hatches in greatest numbers from about the middle of June for three weeks or so. Though *P. horticola* is unknown here, we do have an equivalent June bug (but we would have to call it the December bug), namely the green beetle. Both proliferate in astounding numbers in some seasons. Courtney Williams describes several hundred yards of beach at Fairbourne, Merionethshire, as being thickly carpeted with countless thousands of beetles, a phenomenon not uncommon at the other end of the world when our equivalent enjoys a good year.

Both are terrestrials, and although neither constitutes a major item of trout food for very long, it's the prudent flyfisher who carries an acceptable artificial or two against the day when trout are greedily concentrating on the naturals.

Acceptable artificials of the coch y bonddu plainly feel much at home in New Zealand: everyone speaks highly of them, although not everyone dresses them alike. But then, despite being assured that all the different names for the coch y bonddu in Britain are indeed descriptive of just the one natural, one comes across different dressings for individual alternative names from time to time. Our own disagreement on the dressing isn't much to write home about: some like gold tags and some don't. Oddly, both camps are quite sternly divided on the point, which only goes to show the extraordinary diversity of troutfishing rather than of troutfishers.

Setting aside the similarity of beetle dressings generally (a similarity which might suggest that you really don't need more than one pattern), it's plain that the well-equipped angler here in New Zealand should carry two patterns, one to simulate the green beetle and one the brown beetle, the first with the iridescent green herl of the peacock, and the other with the gleaming bronze herl of the same bird. These two will thus meet the requirements of a green beetle fall or a brown beetle fall. Further, the Coch y Bonddu pattern will double for several other terrestrials, and at a pinch for one or two adult aquatics too. No matter that *Phyllopertha horticola* isn't a resident: George Ferris voted it second place on his list of four best evening and night flies on the river; Norman Marsh believes it to be one of the best all-round patterns ever devised; Keith Draper likes it too; and Hugh McDowell calls it the finest choice when the green beetle is falling on the water. Try double-hackling for best 'buzz' effect.

David Collyer's dressing is:
Hook: 12-14 up-eye
Silk: Black
Tag: Flat gold tinsel or Lurex (fine)
Body: Strands of bronze peacock herl over wet varnish
Hackle: Coch y bonddu.

Because of the great popularity of the fly, the distinctive hackle colour itself became known as coch y bonddu, too, meaning, roughly, red and black. True coch y bonddu hackles (by recent common consent red with black centres and black tips to the fibres) have become extremely rare, and it has been suggested that the name 'furnace' (red with black centre only) should replace the historic Welsh name — just as furnace hackles themselves have replaced coch y bonddu hackles on this and other patterns.

Lastly, the name coch y bonddu never seems to be spelt the same two years running. I have used the version recommended by Eric Horsfall Turner.

COCH Y BONDDU

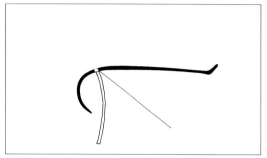

At bend tie in a strip of flat, gold tinsel for tag.

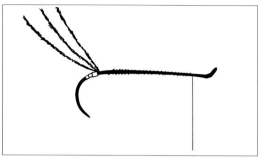

Wrap tinsel around hook. Tie in peacock herls and wind thread to eye.

Make body by wrapping peacock herls over wet varnish applied to hook. Tie in hackle.

Wind on hackle and finish as normal.

12
PYE'S SEDGE

Alan Pye and his wife Leila only just managed to have their refurbished and enlarged Huka Lodge ready for the first of their guests when the Taupo trout season opened on November 1, 1935. Leila was exhausted, but at least everything was spick and span, even if the smell of new paint and varnish lingered unpleasantly everywhere.

This was going to be their sixth season at Huka Lodge. The world had beaten a path to their secluded door right from their modest beginnings in 1930. At Pye's Camp, as some still called that riverside haven of 30 acres of private land along the Waikato River, upstream of Huka Falls, rainbows averaged 7lb, and liked nothing better than a Pye's Sedge, especially well after dark,

Indeed 7lb *was* the average weight of rod-caught rainbows there in the 1930s. Alan Pye's personal best tipped the scales at almost twice the average. If you take a few minutes now in Taupo to inspect the exhibits in the Taupo Regional Museum in Story Place, little more than a stone's throw from the Waikato River itself, you will soon find a large rainbow trout in a glass case. The inscription records the successful angler as Alan Pye and the weight at 13 ½ lb, or a little over 6 kilograms.

It would be entirely appropriate for Pye to have hooked that fish on one of his own sedges, and indeed he probably did; but no-one knows at this distance in time exactly what pattern brought about that specimen rainbow's downfall.

We only know that this man Alan Pye, who loved the world to think he came from Ireland, took his fly-rod down to the river one day and came back with a real giant of a rainbow trout. Only one of his guests, his friend Jack Butland, came close to landing a rainbow from the Huka Lodge water of comparable size. Butland's fish weighed 12 ½ lb, or not quite 6 kg.

The years between 1931 and 1941 at Huka Lodge proved bewilderingly successful for Alan and Leila Pye. In spite of the hard work and long hours

TAKEN by ALAN PYE
WAIKATO RIVER at
HUKA LODGE - 1939
Weight 13½ lb.
Length 26½ ins.
Girth 21½ ins.

demanded by the lodge and its guests in those early years, this man from Cheshire and this woman from Tasmania looked back later on that decade as the happiest period of their lives.

Alan Pye's skill with the fly-rod, and his growing confidence as host in the presence of his mainly titled or celebrated or wealthy or distinguished guests, coupled with his shy wife's reputation as an excellent cook, went much of the way towards making the lodge so well known. Its peaceful setting close to — but not too close to — the main highway between Auckland and Wellington, in grounds which became recognised and respected as a sanctuary for public figures of all kinds while they relaxed for a few days out of the limelight, contributed greatly to the appeal of the lodge.

Day in and day out the deep clear waters of the Waikato River surged past at a constant level and pace on their way from Lake Taupo to Port Waikato 350km north. And constantly throughout the summer and early autumn of that memorable decade, rainbow trout sought stream flies by day and by night, but especially by night.

By the middle of the 1930s, when Alan and Leila took up an option to buy the lodge property after having leased it from the owner, Mrs. Grierson of Wairakei, for five years, the would-be Irishman was known as one of the finest fishermen in New Zealand. And by the end of 1936, the well-respected British tackle firm of Ogden-Smith's in London was recommending its clients who travelled overseas for their trout and salmon fishing to stay at Huka Lodge for superb dry-fly fishing for rainbows. The firm tied and marketed thousands of trout-flies every year, and in 1936 they registered three new patterns at their fly-tying establishment in Croydon; Pye's Nymph, Pye's Brown Nymph, and Pye's Sedge.

I know this through the kindness of Robert Bragg of Christchurch, New Zealand, an Englishman who emigrated here in 1939 after working for some years at Ogden-Smith's Shop at 62 St James' Street, London. Mr Bragg naturally had access to the file of overseas-fishing information which Ogden-Smith's kept updated for clients. Before he emigrated, Robert Bragg made copies of the particular references which would be useful to him in New Zealand. Among them, the magazine articles or notes of Mr Ashley-Dodd, Lieut.-Col. Ross, T.H. Galbraith and others, revealed much of the Taupo trout-fishing scene of those days, and especially of the incredibly-rewarding waters of the Waikato River. Those brief notes on New Zealand's fishing, perused so many times by the eager Robert Bragg that surely he must have known them by heart, recorded the experiences of a mainly wealthy and leisured class of Englishman. Many of those clients of Ogden-Smith's had made regular pilgrimages to Taupo over a period of 25 years or more. They used to break their journeys to fish Lake Leake and Great Lake in Tasmania and the famous Shannon Rise to the snowflake caddis moth of those days. They would fish the Traun at Gmunden, Germany, too, where enormous hatches of large sedges drove trout and trout-fishers frantic. One of the artificials the anglers used successfully at Gmunden resembled the Pye's Sedge of the Waikato. Tied simply with a thick dark brown body, and hen pheasant breast feather for hackle, on a size 11 hook, the pattern was no doubt taken for a hatching sedge.

You don't have to delve deeply into angling entomology around the world to discover surprisingly close resemblances among dozens of insect species which might be separated by as much as 20,000 kilometres. So it is quite on the cards that one fly-fisher's imitation of a Waikato sedge should resemble another's imitation which goes down well at Gmunden. You can be sure that those wealthy Englishmen of half a century ago cast their Traun sedges on Waikato waters, and Pye's Sedges on Traun, and found practically no difference in the responses of the trout.

Those wandering anglers of the early days, together with such good keen men as Alan Pye and Captain Richardson of Taupo and Joe Frost of Turangi, brought changes to the method which had long dominated the fishing of the majority throughout the Taupo fishery.

Trout grew so big that men fished for them as for salmon, downstream and across, with big flies or big spinning lures. As the average size of the fish diminished, however, so did the average size and weight of rods and reels and lines and flies. And one or two flyfishers began to fish English sparsely-hackled wet flies upstream, and some even fished dry flies. And among the dry-fly men was Alan Pye, who had been fishing Central North Island trout-waters since about 1923. Certainly, some trout-fishing background of early years, somewhere in Britain, and then in the South Island, shaped this man's approach to tackle and techniques at Taupo. He fished the lure into stream-mouth rips, and along the rivers, as eagerly as anyone else, but when he found the paradise that lay upstream of Huka Falls, and camped there to fish, days at a time, and beheld the spectacle of an evening rise that often lasted well into the small hours of the morning, the dry fly took command. He began to tie mayflies to deceive Waikato river trout, for his fly-tying was motivated by a preference for pretty-looking flies. It wasn't until Dr J.S. Armstrong, the local doctor, whose hobby was entomology, pointed out that Waikato mayflies were uncommon, that Pye reluctantly turned his fly-tying talents to the fashioning of larval and winged stages of the caddis.

Pye and Armstrong were joined in the late 1920s by a third man with an interest in trout-flies. Captain Richardson, an English mining engineer, shared Pye's love of fishing, and Armstrong's fascination with entomology. But while Pye was quite happy to fish wet flies and lures to trout well below the surface, Richardson was only interested in tying and fishing floating patterns. He would tie caricatures on the spot. He had a kind of genius for improvisation. Dr Armstrong told me that Richardson and he one day found a green-beetle 'hatch' in progress. The Captain there and then cut a piece of flax-leaf, somehow folded and trimmed it to shape, pushed a hook through it, and proceeded to catch the next rainbow he found rising.

For all Pye's more catholic tastes, which allowed him to develop patterns imitating underwater stages of the caddis as well as the winged insect, he must have felt the keenest disappointment when Dr Armstrong pointed out the rarity of Waikato mayflies. In fact, the doctor never found a mayfly in the stomach-contents of a Waikato trout.

Instead of the pretty mayfly patterns he would have preferred to tie, based on the British mayflies he remembered from his earlier flyfishing days, Pye was obliged to concentrate on the much less dainty caddis.

Seemingly, the species that hatched in thousands from dusk until the early hours of the morning, summer after summer, was the caddis which is examined in the larval stage elsewhere in this book, *Hydropsyche colonica*, or as we know it nowadays, *Aoteapsyche colonica*.

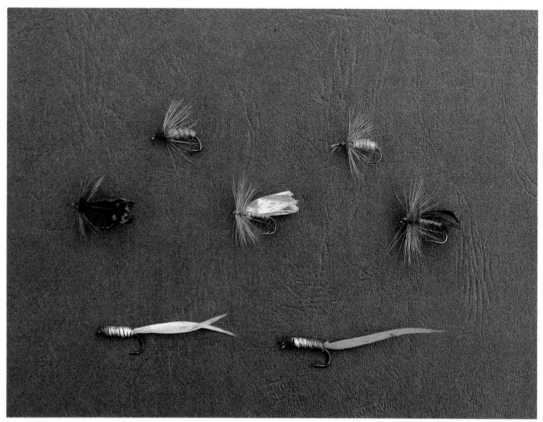

Having hatched from the succession of fast stony rapids upstream, the caddis would swarm to the Huka Lodge lamps, night after night, and in the mornings Leila Pye would have to sweep them up by the bucketful.

Dr Armstrong identified the caddis for his two friends. In the beginning, possibly at the end of the 1920s, it was Captain Richardson who first designed a pattern to imitate the winged caddis. It sat high on the water, and was described to me by Monty Tisdall as the simplest of palmer patterns; just a hook on which hackle was palmered directly to the shank all the way along. The colours were quite bright, one to a fly.

The more I think about such a pattern, the more ludicrous it seems. Why present a thin-bodied but otherwise traditional caterpillar pattern to a trout taking caddis-flies? Surely it couldn't have deceived many trout?

But it did. It worked very well. Captain Richardson's flies were in great demand. Robert Bragg believed that Tisdall's fishing tackle catalogues listed the patterns at some stage, presumably around 1930 or so.

And then Alan Pye introduced a new imitation of the sedge. Moreover, unaffected by Richardson's aversion to wet flies, he designed two larval patterns too.

The new patterns made Richardson's hairy caterpillar look ridiculous.

Pye's conscious effort to dress artificials to resemble a natural fly paid off. His patterns proved gratifyingly successful. Who could doubt a man's fly-designing skills when a prominent British tackle firm seeks permission to register and tie the patterns themselves?

Strangely, however, even the recent change from *Hydropsyche* to *Aoteapsyche* cannot disguise the fact that the colours of the artificial net-builders are all wrong. They don't match up to the naturals. Dr Armstrong somewhat diffidently pointed out to me in 1975 that the coloration of a much less common caddis, *Triplectides obsoleta*, bore a striking resemblance to the artificial *H. colonica* colour scheme . . .

I believe, now, that Alan Pye forbore to model his caddis imitation on the enormously prolific *H. colonica* but chose to copy the long-horn sedge *Triplectides obsoleta* instead. The long-horn is larger and more distinguished-looking than the net-builder. It would have appealed more to Pye's liking for good looks in flies. He probably reasoned, too, that an imitation of the larger and much rarer long-horn would attract immediate attention in a crowd of smaller run-of-the-mill net-builders.

Pye knew from Armstrong that the long-horn did not occupy Waikato waters, at least shortly below Taupo, because the larva needed pieces of reed to burrow into, and reeds did not grow thereabouts. But the long-horn was present around the edges of the lake, and in local streams, and undoubtedly the Waikato rainbows knew it; although the net-builders predominated in stomach-contents, an occasional long-horn would be discovered.

So, although it has been assumed for many years that the most common Waikato caddis-fly of the 1930s and 1940s served as the model for Pye's Sedge, the long-horn, to my mind, exhibits more believable credentials. And yet Jack Butland, later Sir Jack Butland, whose wife Dr Armstrong remembered fly-fishing off the jetty at the entrance of the Taupo boat harbour very early on summer mornings, presented me with a small collection of trout flies, including sedge patterns, tied by Alan Pye himself, and none of them carry the ochreous ginger body of the long-horn. In fact, they look rather like our local net-builders . . .

Officially, in 1936, Ogden-Smith's dressed Pye's Sedge this way:

Hook: 10-14
Silk: Brown
Body: Ostrich dyed to an ochreous shade
Wings: Shag flights, black, tied penthouse style and cut
Hackle: Dark ginger.

PYE'S SEDGE

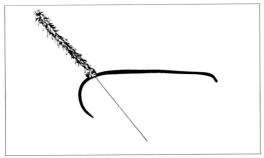

Tie in body ostrich herl at bend. Wind forward to form body.

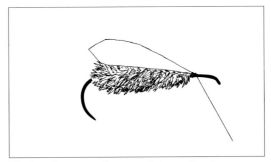

Tie in wings penthouse style and cut.

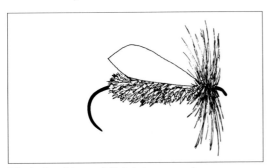

Tie in hackle and finish in normal way.

13
RED PALMER AND THE CATERPILLAR CONNECTION

Whatever may be said about caterpillars as a food of fish, the palmer-flies tied to imitate them have deceived trout for centuries.

G.E.M. Skues had no doubt that palmers "are as often taken for struggling sedge flies as for the woolly bears and other caterpillars they are fancifully supposed to represent". Francis Francis considered that to say a palmer was taken for a caterpillar invaded the realms of fancy. The only occasions on which he could remember seeing a particularly common species on the water was "when I threw it there myself to experimentalise". Francis was having a dig at Alfred Ronalds, the celebrated English angler-entomologist, for seeming to presume that trout receive many opportunities to eat caterpillars. Ronalds' particular favourite was the caterpillar of the garden tiger moth *Arctia caja*, which he found more abundant than any other caterpillar in the spring. He accordingly recommended fishing a Red Palmer to imitate the caterpillar as soon as the water was fit to fish after a flood, and also on windy days.

What a wealth of memories the Red Palmer has bestowed on generations of flyfishers! Right back to the year 1651, when Thomas Barker's *Art of Angling* appeared, and possibly some way beyond that, the Red Palmer, ribbed with gold, has enchanted trout and troutfishers. For one thing, the four palmer flies Barker stipulated served fishermen well all year long, morning and evening, windy or cloudy, he said. Which doesn't sound as though he fished them as caterpillar imitations at all, for most of the year.

But the Red Palmer is still a most popular pattern, and I don't think it will ever go out of fashion.

While the actual pattern indeed goes back well over 300 years, the palmer style of hackling an artificial fly to give it 'buzz' goes back further still, some say to the *Treatise* itself, in the fifteenth century. You wrapped a hackle the full length of the body in those days to make a palmer, and you do exactly the same today. The word 'palmer' is given two meanings in my dictionary, both dating from about the thirteenth century. One has it that pilgrims who customarily carried palm branches as a sign of their visits to the Holy Land were known as palmers, the other that the name was given to the itinerant monks who wandered through the land in those days. The second meaning is readily associated with the many kinds of caterpillar that wander here, there and everywhere. And so they became palmers too, a name which has been handed down to the present day. River and reservoir flyfishers of our time are no less ready to present a Red Palmer, wet or dry, to a feeding trout, than were their counterparts three or more centuries ago.

By common consent over the past hundred years or so, however, insistence on the identity of the original model for the palmer fly has moderated. From the looper-caterpillar, caterpillar, woolly-bear, palmer-worm — and much later the wooly worm of the Americans — our palmer now does duty as an imitation of a dozen foods of trout, among them nymphs, hatching duns, leeches, shrimps, sedges caught in the surface film, and moths and other terrestrials. Some say the caterpillar connection is still very much there, but most anglers realise that, though the little wanderers travel many roads, they rarely walk on water.

Sometimes those tiny pale green grubs found on willow leaves end up in the water below, but never in numbers sufficient to drive waiting trout into feeding frenzies. We have plenty of true caterpillars too, but, like Francis, I can't ever remember seeing one floating on the water, even on streams whose banks are overhung in many places by scrub, hebes, and larger trees. This isn't to say that caterpillars never get into the water. You would think that they're far more likely to make a meal for trout than millipedes, and yet I've caught Waipunga rainbows absolutely crammed with those hard and shiny-brown little arthropods with all the legs, but never a caterpillar.

Nevertheless, so-called caterpillar imitations can often mean the difference between success and failure, but I'm talking chiefly about the Red Palmer itself, a 'portmanteau' imitation if ever there was one. Flyfishers of the exact-imitation school might not like the idea of the general-purpose Red Palmer, but when trout themselves plainly can't tell the difference between a Red Palmer and a hatching sedge, say, or a moth, I see no reason to enlighten them.

All the same, two of the following patterns do deliberately seek to copy grubs and caterpillars; first, the Willow Grub, tied on size 16 or 18 hooks, and second the family of smooth caterpillars, on short-shanked size 12-14 hooks. The Willow Grub is quite simply tied with a pale primrose floss silk body and a dark brown head. Smooth caterpillars in appropriate colours are best styled after Fogg's Chenille Grub imitation. Chenille isn't strictly smooth of course, but no hackle, palmered or otherwise, is embodied. Again, the tie is simplicity itself:

fasten a short length of fine chenille just behind the eye of the hook only, and form a head with the black or dark brown tying silk.

But the *pièce de résistance* is the foundation member of the mock-caterpillar clan, the Red Palmer. In the beginning, and up to about the middle of the last century, peacock herl was always used for the body. Nowadays, red seal's fur or red wool is the preferred alternative. Once again, the dressing is an extremely simple one.

Hook: 8-12
Silk: Red
Body: Red seal's fur or red wool
Hackle: Natural red cock, palmered (seven turns) the length of the body. Use natural red hen for wet version
Ribbing: Flat or oval gold tinsel.

RED PALMER

Tie in body material, ribbing and hackle.

Wind body to eye.

Wind hackle palmer style to eye with seven turns. Wind ribbing through to eye and secure. Tie off and finish in normal way.

14
A QUEEN
OF KAKAHI

Perhaps it is just as well that the family of New Zealand mayflies is not a large one. So far, some 30 species have been identified. More will probably join the list as entomologists push their field researches further and further back into more remote regions of the country.

But, for the time being — and doubtless even if another 30 species are eventually revealed — flyfishers need concern themselves with only about half the number named so far; in other words, only the commonest or most often encountered of the mayflies, or Ephemeroptera, inhabiting our more readily accessible waters.

Of those dozen or more species I meant to single out just one for the purpose of this book and for the interest of flyfishers and fly-tiers: *Coloburiscus humeralis*, the spiny-gilled mayfly, and the dressing devised to imitate both the dun and the spinner of this familiar fly, the pattern known as the Kakahi Queen.

But I found that some flyfishers well versed in New Zealand aquatic insect entomology and fly-dressing might not take kindly to this connection between *C. humeralis* and the Kakahi Queen, although when Norman Marsh published his *Trout Stream Insects of New Zealand*, the link was formalised. Earlier doubts were put to rest. Or were they? The only other book dealing in detail with New Zealand trout-fly imitations and their origins, and in many cases the natural insects on which they are modelled, Keith Draper's *Trout Flies in New Zealand*, attributes *Ameletopsis perscitus* origins to the Kakahi Queen.

A Christchurch angler quoted by Draper, Peter Laing, believed that "one of the best copies of any of our New Zealand mayflies is the Kakahi Queen". Draper mentions confirmation of *A. perscitus* origins for the Kakahi Queen by no less an authority than R.K. Bragg. Laing's quoted opinion can be taken two ways. He could have meant that because the Kakahi Queen was one of the best copies of any one of the mayfly species it could be used with confidence to represent whatever mayfly was on the water at the time. But a further remark of his does tend to identify his earlier opinion with *A. perscitus*, so we may take it that he is praising the artificial for its role as an *A. perscitus* imitation.

Now, Draper's was the only authoritative and extensively published angling voice on New Zealand trout-flies before Marsh came along 12 years later, in 1983, with his sumptuous book about trout stream insects and their imitation.

So who had decided between Draper in 1971 and Marsh in 1983 that the Kakahi Queen was now a *Coloburiscus humeralis* and not an *Ameletopsis perscitus* imitation? When had the consensus Draper talks about translated into an apparently quite new Marsh consensus? And if you are familiar with Marsh's book you may well ask on whose authority does Marsh additionally assign *Nesameletus* species to Kakahi Queen origins?

Actually, of course, such matters are of concern chiefly to entomologist-anglers and fly-tying historians. And anyway, nomenclature and description have tended to become, if not confused, then certainly confusing. Old names and new, old descriptions and new, draw attention to several likenesses among the species, notably likenesses expressed by the entomologists. So the possibility of anglers themselves confusing one species with another is very real.

But if entomologist-anglers and fly-tying specialists like Draper or Marsh haven't the authority to name and attribute origins to the artificials that appear over the horizon every so often, who on earth in New Zealand has?

Much much earlier than either Draper or Marsh, an English flyfisher, Dr J.C. Mottram, visiting here in 1911, wedded an extensive knowledge of aquatic and terrestial insects taken by trout to a gifted enthusiast's talent for fly-tying. As long ago as 1915, in his book *Fly Fishing; Some New Arts and Mysteries*, Mottram published the first popular description of several New Zealand mayflies, gave them names of his own, and devised dressings for them. Among them was one he called the Great Pepper-winged, the mayfly *Coloburiscus humeralis*, which he dressed somewhat differently from the patterns which evolved later under the name of Kakaki Queen.

Mottram did not list *Ameletopsis perscitus* (in his day it appears to have been known as *Ameletus perscitus*), or *Nesameletus* species, although our own G.V. Hudson had dealt with them both, as well as other mayflies apparently unknown to Mottram, in his book *New Zealand Neuroptera*, published seven years before Mottram visited.

Mottram's dry-fly dressings of 1915 met with as little acclaim here as the series of five wet-fly patterns which Captain Hamilton gave us in the same year that Hudson's book appeared. No-one ties them commercially now — although the so-called Captain Hamilton hook itself is curently fashionable. Not the flies.

Sadly in some ways, only three named home-grown patterns designed to imitate New Zealand mayflies have enjoyed a widespread following and lasting success here. Tony Orman, in *The Sport in Fishing,* comments, "Except for the odd New Zealand creation, most notably the Kakahi Queen (what a beautiful creature, yet so realistic) fly-fishermen have stuck with traditional British patterns . . ."

Two of our creations evolved at Kakahi; The Kakahi Queen, and the Twilight Beauty. Together with the Dad's Favourite they have become a tiny island in the huge sea of British and American patterns which have swamped our tackle shops for years.

For two of the three well-known New Zealand patterns to have come out of the small township called Kakahi, close to the Whakapapa River in the King Country, is remarkable enough, but for both to have been designed by one man, the local postmaster Basil Humphrey, or Humphries, speaks volumes for the man's inventiveness.

Greg Kelly, in his delightful book *The Flies in My Hat,* tells the story of the Twilight Beauty and also of another pattern (or rather a series of patterns) the Jessie, with which the Kakahi postmaster is also credited and which itself is not exactly unknown to New Zealand flyfishers. He talks of the Kakahi Queen too, but his information at the time, which came to him from the woman for whom the Jessie had been named fifty years earlier, in 1917, Mrs. Mont-Brown, was incomplete. Mrs. Mont-Brown had written to tell Kelly about the origins of the Twilight Beauty and the Jessie. He said that although she stated that the Kakahi Queen had been a very popular pattern in the Kakahi district for many years she did not claim that it had been the work of the same group, headed by Mr. Humphrey, that produced the other patterns.

However, by the time *Trout Flies in New Zealand* was published, four years after *The Flies in My Hat,* Keith Draper had ascertained, presumably in conversation with Greg Kelly, that the Kakahi postmaster had indeed invented the pattern himself. Kelly, who knew little about entomology, and did not tie his own flies, knew that the natural was common on the Whakapapa but could not be certain of its identity.

Solving the riddle of the Kakahi Queen's derivation is too esoteric an exercise for most. But wouldn't it be wonderful to be able to arrange a day's fishing on the Whakapapa River of old, at Kakahi, for Basil Humphrey, G.V. Hudson, Greg Kelly, Keith Draper and Norman Marsh? The secret would be out in a jiffy.

No matter; like Sawyer's Pheasant Tail Nymph — which itself successfully impersonates several species of mayfly nymphs, including New Zealand ones — we'll have to allow the Kakahi Queen's cloak to be spread over several naturals, but particularly those duns or spinners with yellow about the wings.

First, there's *Ameletopsis perscitus*, widely distributed in stony streams but never common. Hudson called it very pretty, noted the pale ochreous body of the spinner with its series of pale brown markings and black dots on the back. The wings, he said, are a "bright clear yellow and very shining".

Coloburiscus humeralis, too, is widely distributed in stony streams, but much more common than *A.perscitus*. Marsh describes the imago as having a dark fawn body with brown banding, and pale primrose-tinted transparent wings.

The two *Nesameletus* species *ornatus* and *flavitinctus* are widely distributed in stony streams too. They are practically indistinguishable. Hudson found that the spinner of *ornatus* very closely resembled that of *C. humeralis*. The body is an olive-fawn colour, the wings greyish with yellow fore-edges.

Whichever one of those four naturals you plump for, the Kakahi Queen will make a look-alike convincing enough for most trout. And you have basically two patterns to chose from, Draper's and Marsh's. Draper does give an alternative dressing which was favoured in Canterbury at the time his book was published. But he points out that R.K. Bragg (himself a Canterbury man) nevertheless preferred the Kakahi postmaster's pattern.

And that pattern, as Draper gives it in *Trout Flies in New Zealand*, tied wet or dry on hooks size 10-14, is:

Body: Stripped peacock herl quill
Wing: Mallard duck fronted with mallard breast dyed yellow
Hackle: Golden furnace (Greenwell's)
Whisks: As hackle.

Marsh recommends hook sizes 12-14, and his dressing for the floating artificial only is:

Body: Well marked stripped peacock eye quill
Hackle: Brown or dark ginger cock. Add dyed yellow cock if unwinged
Wings: Grey mallard with dyed yellow partridge
Tail: Brown or ginger cock.

That wise old angler George Ferris said of the Kakahi Queen, way back in the 1960s, that the pattern was one of the most scientific imitations. When kept to size 16 or 14, he said, it can be relied upon and fished with confidence.

Hook: 12-16
Silk: Medium brown
Tail: Furnace or coch y bonddu fibres
Body: Well-marked stripped peacock quill
Wings: Grey mallard fronted with mallard or partridge dyed yellow
Hackle: Furnace or coch y bonddu. Front with dyed yellow cock if unwinged.

KAKAHI QUEEN

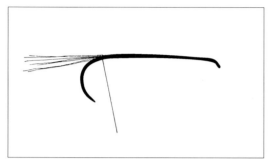

Tie in whisks of hackle for tail.

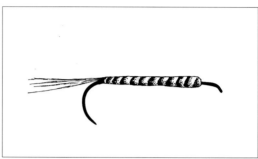

Tie in and wind on stripped peacock eye quill to position for wings.

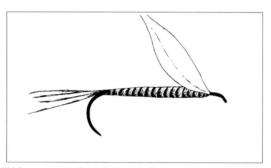

Wings are tied in upright position, placing yellow part of wing to front.

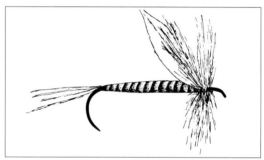

Finish by tying in hackle and tying off in normal fashion.

15
CASE FOR
CADDIS

Early one morning alongside the
Hydro Pool on the Tongariro, I watched a heron unhurriedly winkling morsels
out of a flood-puddle. The river had come up quickly the previous evening after
some hours of rain, and had just as quickly dropped again overnight. Now,
bankside vegetation wore a brushed-back look, and here and there a flood-
puddle sparkled in the morning sunshine.

Curious to see what the stooped grey bird with the long bill was finding to
eat, I moved closer, suddenly mindful that flood-puddles often reveal much of
great interest to human stream-fishers — provided they get to them before their
avian counterparts.

I vividly recall the trout-food secret laid bare by a small Hutt River flood-
puddle just below the old concrete bridge at Akatarawa. As I passed by, small
flickers of movement caught my eye, and I knelt down to investigate.

Twenty or more nymphs were trapped in the puddle. They were all mature
nymphs of the mayfly *Zephlebia cruentata* (now renamed *Acanthophlebia cruentata)*. I had never suspected their presence in the river, and yet here were 20 which
had been washed from their moorings by a fresh and swept together into a small
backwater sanctuary which was even then in the process of draining slowly
away. If only I had known of the existence of those orange-red nymphs, I might
have improved my catch-rate of browns from the Hutt. As it was, I was soon to
move to Taupo, and *Zephlebia cruentata* imitations for the Wellington area were
never tied.

When the heron reluctantly lifted himself on slow wings and abandoned
the Tongariro flood-puddle that morning, I approached his tiny pond with some
interest.

He had been making inroads into a stranded population of the net-building
caddis *Hydropsyche colonica* (now renamed *Aoteapsyche colonica)*. Scores of them

96

remained. They were not very happy. Some were beyond caring. Many had life enough left in them to crawl slowly around. They would die before long because these net-builders of the caddis world need moving water to survive. Each builds a tiny net to catch food particles brought down by the current (or by moving water at the edges of some lakes). When a rush of water grows too strong for them, however, the larvae and their nets get washed away. Bowling along, many caddis quickly end up inside waiting trout. Others sweep into new quarters downstream. Some drift into miniature backwaters which the flooded river abandons once the level drops.

That Tongariro flood-puddle was an eye-opener. Ever since that morning, the net-building caddis has loomed large on my fishing horizons. Not only on Tongariro, but also on Tauranga-Taupo and Hinemaiaia, and on other rivers in the region, imitations of the larval stage of *Aoteapsyche colonica* have become obligatory patterns. Time and again they have vindicated the priority I allocate to them. One year I fished with virtually nothing else.

True, I kept no records of those 12 months of Taupo fishing trips. But that year, mainly on Tongariro and Hinemaiaia, I proved to myself that, if you like fishing the nymph, you need nothing more than imitations of the net-building caddis larva to take good fish through the season. I suspect that the same prescription is true all over the country, for the net-builders are widely distributed.

My year of *H. colonica* came to an end at an appropriate stage in the evolving world of the entomologists. For suddenly the name *Hydropsyche* itself came to an end. Henceforth, said the pundits, *Hydropsyche* would become *Aoteapsyche*. Why the change? Was it in response to the need to bring more Maori language into our lives? I am a little sad about the matter. The new name doesn't trip off the tongue as happily as the old. My Latin pronunciation may be at fault, but I always pronounced the old name as "hydro-sikey-colonnica", and so, apparently, did the anonymous author of a limerick which appeared in an early issue of the newsletter of the Taupo Fly-fishers' Club:

> If more *Hydropsyche colonica*
> Were commonly found in Lake Wanaka,
> I'd nymph Glendhu Bay
> With the caddis all day,
> And at night swig the old *Ginantonica*

Somehow, the new name doesn't scan in that verse. And quite apart from that, what could have been more appropriate than to have discovered the prevalence of Tongariro *Hydropsyche colonica* at the Hydro Pool?

Few flyfishers anywhere should consider themselves well equipped who don't carry imitations of the larva of the local net-builder. Whether in the United States, or Canada, or Britain, or Australia, as well as New Zealand, Hydropsychidae are legion. They have great significance everywhere. For instance, H.H. Ross, in *The Caddis Flies or Trichoptera of Illinois*, says that the Hydropsychidae caddises are the most abundant faunal element in most of the rivers and streams of the Midwest. Larry Solomon and Eric Leiser, in their *The Caddis and the Angler*, say that the Hydropsychidae are the most common of all caddis. Writing of stream insects in his *New Zealand Neuroptera*, G.V. Hudson was saying as long ago as 1904 that the net-builder is a favourite article of food with the trout, and "as it occurs in large numbers during the winter and is full grown in the very early spring, it must be an important item in the dietary of that fish". Another entomologist, R.J. Tillyard, gave it as his opinion that *A. colonica* is easily the commonest caddis-fly in New Zealand.

In case you need more convincing that this insect is really important, one other fact will surely persuade you: larvae of all sizes up to 20mm in length are found throughout the year. Adult imitations may therefore be fished confidently at any time.

One man who once, and once only, fished a caddis larva with extraordinary success in England was G.E.M. Skues. So deadly did his imitation prove that he gave up fishing it after just a few minutes. His conscience wouldn't allow him to keep on catching fish on his "caddis or gentle". He left us dozens of excellent nymph and other fly patterns, but he wouldn't reveal the tying of either his caddis or his equally successful alder-fly larva imitation.

A gentle (blowfly maggot) is perhaps not greatly different from a caddis larva, and Skues just wasn't going to insult his gentlemanly chalkstream trout with patterns imitative of one or the other. At this distance it seems odd that a man who espoused the nymph should shrink from using the caddis larva. Both naturals become stream-flies, and Skues was as ready to fish a sedge as a mayfly: it all depended on the preference of the fish at the time.

I have gone to some lengths to emphasize the importance of the net-building caddis because I am absolutely convinced that, unless the angler claims a Skues-like distaste for the business, he would do well to fish imitations of the caddis larva far more often.

But I am talking about honest-to-goodness imitations, not the white blowfly maggot imitations currently popular on the Tongariro. Perhaps I seem as illogical as Skues, but when we are flyfishing for trout, whether rainbows or browns, and offering them fly-imitations, I know there's far more satisfaction, far more pleasure, far more skill, in the successful presentation of a pattern genuinely impersonating some stage of a local stream-fly than in fishing some garish concoction bearing no resemblance to anything aquatic.

Flyfishers wanting to add net-building caddis imitations to their armouries had first better catch themselves some naturals from the waters they normally fish, simply to match the colours of their artificials to them. Colours vary from water to water. That phenomenon characterises most stream insects, and anglers who take advantage of that knowledge are going to succeed more often than those who stick to published-pattern shades.

I could never understand why Keith Draper seemed a bit diffident about tying me up a supply of *Olinga feredayi*, for which I wrote out a description. I had no idea, then, having just moved to Taupo, that the horny-cased caddis familiar to me from the Hutt River differed so much from its Taupo counterpart. It wasn't until I killed my first Waipunga trout and found it full of a dull little caricature of the Hutt's bright *O. feredayi* that I began to understand Keith's diffidence.

The same refusal to wear exactly the same colours everywhere is true of *A. colonica* too. Entomologists and anglers describe the heads and the tops of the first three body-segments as black, or dark brown. That is, some say black and some say brown. One colour is close enough to the other not to send a trout flying for its life, but it does seem that the body-colour varies considerably and should be carefully considered. Tongariro specimens are a grubby light brown tinged with green. Norman Marsh, in his *Trout Stream Insects of New Zealand*, recommends a body dubbed with the grey-blue under-fur of a hare. Pye's Nymph, which Keith Draper says in his *Trout Flies in New Zealand* was designed to simulate the rising pupa of one of the Hydropsychidae, should apparently be dressed with a ginger-coloured wool. Hudson described the body of the natural as dull greenish-brown. A fisherman who telephoned me about the pattern one day from Pahiatua said that the net-builders in his district were definitely grey.

Whatever shade or shades you actually settle for, spare a thought for the shape of the artificial as well. Larvae of the net-builders, once torn from their homes, assume a curved shape. Solomon and Leiser say that the convex surface forms the back and concave surface the belly. Robert H. Boyle and Dave Whitlock, in *The Fly-Tyer's Almanac*, imply the importance of that curve by tying larval imitations on English bait hooks, sizes 12 and 14.

Commending Solomon and Leiser's book and patterns, Gary Borger, in *Nymphing: A Basic Book*, recommends stressing the strong segmentation of the abdomen and the dark thorax, short legs, and colour of the natural, and advises showing the pronounced abdominal gilling.

Inevitably, a few New Zealand dressings have been developed since R. McLachlan first recorded *H. colonica* in 1871; and obviously other dressings have evolved overseas, especially in the United States.

In addition to the ginger pupa dressing for Pye's Nymph given by Keith Draper in 1971, and Tony Orman's Raffia Nymph and Cream Caddis noted in the revised paperback edition of his *Trout with Nymph*, published in 1983, *A. colonica* emerges, under Norman Marsh's direction, in 1983, as the Woolly Caddis. Marsh specifies caddis hooks of sizes 14-16, black head and thorax, the grey-blue under-fur of a hare for the body, and legs of ginger hen. Wise in the ways of trout, Marsh remarks that the pattern is most useful during early season, when above-normal flow conditions apply, "Many 'woollies' are then disturbed and trout are quick to take advantage. A few turns of lead wire prior to tying can then be a decided advantage in getting the fly down into that most productive of all areas, the stream bed". How right he is!

My own pattern, tied for the Taupo area, differs little from Marsh's, but I do like to stress the segmentation of the natural, the distinctive dorsal or upper coloration of the forward third of the larva, and the fattish appearance of the central section of the body.

The American Polly Rosborough published a book in 1965 called *Tying and Fishing the Fuzzy Nymphs.* In it he describes the making of 'noodles', those rolled lengths of fur, tapered at both ends, which are wound on to form the bodies of many of his patterns.

Nowadays, with an old Southern song in mind, I can't dissociate Polly from

Polly Wolly *Noodle* rather than Polly Wolly *Doodle*, which is a constant reminder that the American steered me into a technique wonderfully well adapted to the making of bodies suitably bulbous in the right places.

A noodle of opossum fur simulates the soft body of the caddis very well. Choose a dull light-brown colour, roll several noodles of sizes appropriate to the hooks you want to dress, and tease out the same number and length of 'pieces' of green Polyblende.

Lay a noodle on a base of filmy Polyblende and roll them together. The result achieves the grubby brown colour, tinged with green, of the Tongariro caddis. Tie the head and upper surface of the body for a quarter of its length with black tying silk and black floss silk or possum tail. Deliberately emphasised segmentation is important. In the early days I simulated the segments with dark green tying thread. I still think that colour looks best, but for some time now I have substituted flat gold tinsel for the green silk and it works well.

It would be good to tie these *A. colonica* imitations entirely without weight for the Tongariro, but in many pools and reaches the angler needs to sink his artificials to the depth at which trout are lying. Especially when they're running up the rivers, the trout hug the bottom.

At present, you may fish weighted artificials on hooks up to and including size 8 in the Taupo Fishing District. It is possible to load a fair amount of lead or copper wire on an 8 hook, but the heavier you make it the more difficult it is to cast. Particularly in the running season, weight built into nymphs appears essential to success, but it was only a few years ago that many of us fished the Tongariro and other local rivers with unweighted nymphs and landed more fish than we do today.

Because the natural assumes a curved shape when tumbling downstream, it's best to tie artificials on caddis hooks or English bait hooks. For the Tongariro, size 10s are quite big enough, but the smaller sizes suggested by Marsh and Boyle are more appropriate for smaller waters.

If you tie the pattern with a fur dubbing (rather than the latex which some tiers recommend), you can add a finishing touch which may mean the difference between failure and success some days. One of the distinctive characteristics of the Hydropsychidae is the heavy gilling along the lower sides of the larva. This has the appearance of fringes of short hair. You can imitate the fringes by picking out tufts of fur with a dubbing needle.

One last point. Although there appear to be no mentions in the New Zealand literature, some American writers draw attention to the silk thread 'lifeline' of certain caddises, including net-builders, and the desirability of imitating them. No doubt our own Hydropsychidae spin and rely on lifelines too, like astronauts taking walks in space, and it may be that imitating the lifeline

could add more credence to the artificial. The Americans achieve the results they want by colouring the last few inches of the tippet with a white felt pen.

Hook: 10-14 caddis or baithook
Silk: Olive
Body: Fur or wool
Ribbing: Flat gold tinsel.

CADDIS

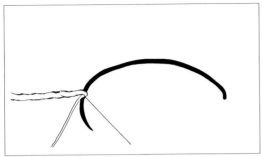

Tie in body material and tinsel for ribbing.

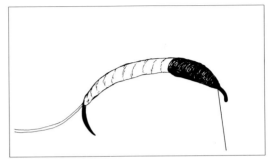

Wind to form body. Tie head and thorax and tie off.

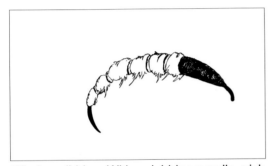

Wind on ribbing. With a dubbing needle, pick out tufts of fur on underside.

16
TINY TERRESTRIAL

If you have read Arthur Ransome's *Rod and Line* you will know his account of an experience with winged ants. They invaded his home. It occurred to him that they must be models clamouring for a sitting, so he popped one in a glass test tube and set up his fly-tying gear. Before attempting a pattern, you will remember, he conferred with the Old Masters, to compare their dressings with the natural insect. He went back a long way.

In fact, writers in English who talk of winged ants for angling go back to the Dame herself, who wrote her treatise in the early years of the 15th century. As far as the scholars know, she gave no dressing for the ant among her twelve flies for trout, simply naming the natural fly as a bait for chub and dace in July.

Her successors did give dressings, among them the author of the first known essay on fly-fishing, Charles Cotton, who listed 65 fly patterns in his *Instructions How to Angle for Trout and Grayling in a Clear Stream*, which appeared for the first time in 1676 as the second part of Izaak Walton's fifth edition of *The Complete Angler*.

Cotton's flies for June included a flying ant dressed with a mixed dubbing of brown and red camlet (a soft wool) and a light grey wing; and for August one dressed with "a dubbing of the black-brown hair of a cow, some red warped in for the tag of his tail, and a dark wing".

Ransome, exploring the dressings of Ronalds, Pulman, Theakston, Francis, Pritt, Edmonds and Lee, and West, was struck by the frequency with which peacock herl was specified for the body material. Even the ruddiest bronze herl, he felt, could hardly give the luminous chestnut or the apparent hardness of the actual insect.

Although Leonard West gives peacock as an alternative dressing for a dry fly, Halford forbore to specify the material for the dry Brown Ant included as No. 28 of his new series of exact imitations of those days. This was the pattern the great dry-fly man must have developed from a painstaking examination of the many live ants he captured one August afternoon of 1903 on the Itchen at St Cross. He was there to fish; suddenly an unprecedented flight of ants occurred, driving the trout into the normal feeding frenzy of trout at such times; and yet Halford resisted the temptation to make a record bag, and lay aside his rod to spend several hours securing as many live ants as possible.

Ransome doesn't sound particularly impressed by the dressing. Leonard West's, he feels, is much more like the insect. But the dressing he believed a great improvement on all the others was that of J.W. Dunne, of *Sunshine and the Dry Fly* fame, who advocated white-painted hooks to impart translucence to the bodies of artificial flies.

Dressed with artificial silk on a white-painted hook, with hackle-pointed wings laid flat, and a dark honey hackle, Dunne's pattern, said Ransome, was so good it was not likely to be superseded. And I know why he thought that, and I shall explain a little later on.

In the meantime, though, it must be said that Dunne's dressing has been superseded. All kinds of patterns have evolved over the years, and all tied to meet that rare emergency when ants are on the water. Accept that the wingless variety falls from overhanging vegetation much more often than we suppose, and that imitations are consequently likely to be accepted with alacrity. Certainly a flight of winged ants across the water, however, doesn't very often coincide with a fishing trip. When it does, though, on still, sultry, humid summer days, you will have an urgent need of two or three artificials.

These flights of migrating ants occur all over the world. Troutfishers are either driven to exaltation or exasperation, according to whether or not they carry ant imitations. For invariably the trout abandons whatever other food it may be taking at the time and gorges on ants. Often, the occasion won't last long, but if you knot on an ant pattern quickly and the naturals aren't too thick on the water, sport can be fast and furious. David Collyer one afternoon at Blagdon, responding immediately to such a situation, landed eight fish in half an hour.

Trout obviously like ants, and this is strange. It has been known for a very long time that the insects have formic acid in them, and formic acid is, according to my dictionary, a "colourless corrosive liquid carboxylic acid". It's an acid that smells like urine, hence Dame Juliana's references in her treatise, not to ants, but, in the vernacular of her day, to pysmires, meaning urinating ants, from the smell characteristic of anthills (which are occasionally known as formicaria).

E.R. Hewitt, incidentally, claimed that trout preferred ants to any other food and would always turn to them when available — because of their acidic taste.

So far, mention has been made of the winged ant, the flying ant, the Brown

Ant of Halford. There's the Red Ant and the Black Ant to be considered too — the popular names given to English ants — and to American ants for that matter: Schwiebert's *Matching the Hatch* ant imitations, for instance, comprise the Black Ant, the Red Ant, the Black Flying Ant, and the Red Flying Ant, the latter two fished either wet or dry. Sizes 10-14, fished in the surface film, are deadly, says Schwiebert, and, according to Charles Fox, Ernest's favourite imitation has a black seal's fur body and blue-grey wing.

Besides seal's fur, ant dressings have featured pig's wool, floss silk, deer hair, cork, nylon monofilament, latex, fur, deep orange silk, peacock herl, tying silk varnished until smooth. So a lot of experimentation and much thought have been expended on this small terrestrial and its imitation.

Two of the characteristics of this and other land-based insects make tying and fishing the terrestrials 'dry' a relatively simple affair. Whereas the final winged stage of aquatic insects impresses us with its delicacy and translucence, terrestrials are usually bulky, opaque creatures. Furthermore, unlike the mayflies, for instance, which perch daintily on the surface film, terrestrials fall part-way through. True, they float, at least for a time, but they float in the surface, not on it. Artificials should be floated in the film the same way. They can be made to ride desirably low by trimming hackle away on the underside in the shape of a V.

Another benefit of fishing terrestrials was implied by the famous American angler-entomologist and fly-tier Preston Jennings, when he gave it as his opinion that brown trout taking land insects are not all that selective. And he's right. Many New Zealand brown trout are as fastidious as any of the breed when offered representations of aquatic insects. But whack a big Cicada down on the water at the right time of year and they rush it open-mouthed.

It sounded as though Arthur Ransome encouraged some brown trout into similar enthusiasm the day the winged ants invaded his home. Having tied half a dozen artificials to Dunne's instructions, he oiled them and went off to the river. The first ant had hardly floated six inches when a trout had it. Ransome landed 11 more. No wonder he thought the world of Dunne's dressing.

Ants can be tied just hackled, but it does seem the fashion to wing them for those occasions when the winged naturals are falling on the water. Possibly, anglers feel that an insect floating in the film, perhaps on its side, can be more closely and critically examined than a mayfly, say, which stands up on tiptoe. But against that we have Preston Jennings' opinion, and of course it would be true that hackled flies generally are more popular than winged ones, and perform equally well. My own preference is for flies without separate feather wings, but in the case of the ant, the traditional two hackle tips, tied flat over the back, do not unduly complicate manufacture and may at times add just that extra touch of realism and trigger a response.

Decisions on body colours are easy enough to make; with red, black and brown artificials the angler is well-equipped anywhere. Many of our own 33 species are dressed in those colours, although a reddish-yellow shade is not unknown in some.

For want of a home-grown New Zealand pattern, I have gone to one of the American dressings, Poul Jorgensen's, given in his contribution to J. Michael Migel's book *The Masters on the Dry Fly*. It's nice and simple, but I must say I don't like the idea of going down to size 28 hooks. Match all materials to the body colour of the ant being imitated.

Hook: 10-28
Body: Two clumps of fur, the rear larger than the front
Hackle: Tied sparsely between the two fur clumps and trimmed top and bottom.

ANT

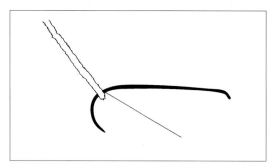

Tie in body material at bend.

Form first part of body shape and tie in hackle.

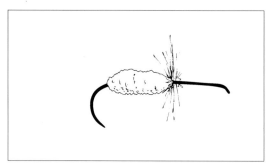

Wind hackle around hook and tie off.

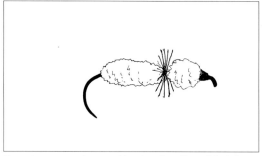

Create second part of body, tie off and finish as normal. Cut hackle back to just above body depth.

17
DEADLY DRAGON

A journey through the popular en-
tomological and angling literature of the dragonfly leads you to some remarkable facts and some memorable stories.

One of the stories I like best is Dr J.C. Mottram's, the one he relates in the
book that Arnold Gingrich thought so highly of: *Fly-fishing: Some New Arts and
Mysteries*, published as long ago as 1915, some four years after Dr Mottram came
to New Zealand to fish and quietly and thoughtfully and comprehensively go
about solving, one after the other, all the trout-catching puzzles awaiting him
here.

His talk of dragonflies concerns a time he spent fishing certain small spring-
fed creeks crossing the Canterbury Plains. Arriving at the spring-head pools, he
would find scores of little red dragonflies skimming about. A puff of wind would
cast some of the flies on the water, and then would come several bold rises of fine
fish. Having no imitation dragonflies with him on the first occasion, he tried large
dry flies on the fish, but with no success.

Then, being an unusually well-prepared dry-fly and nymph fisherman
from the chalk streams of the south of England, he pulled out his pocket fly-tying
gear and set about tying little-red-dragonfly imitations on the spot. He made a
head and thorax of red wool, used a grass straw as a detached body, tied in wings
of white hackle tips, and wound a turn or two of badger hackle for legs. The
doctor wrote: "On the first cast of this a thick four-pounder laid hold, and,
subsequently, others showed their appreciation of it."

We can assume that this was the pattern that other trout much further north
showed appreciation of too; and I suspect that the stream was the Tokaanu
Stream, in the days before it was closed to all fishing. Dr Mottram was not an
admirer of the overall rainbow-trout fishery he found at Taupo, but he thoroughly enjoyed the little spring-fed stream, close to the Tongariro, in which he

hooked 11 rainbows between two and four pounds each one day, most of them on dragonfly imitations.

Mottram's experience of trout eager for his winged dragonflies (damselflies, though, I suspect) is at odds with A. Courtney Williams' evaluation of the worth of winged patterns fished dry. And what about that incredible story George Ferris tells us in *The Trout are Rising*, the one about lake-dwelling browns and rainbows leaping clean out of the water to take large dragonflies in rapid flight? On the one hand, Ferris bears out Courtney Williams by assuring us that "the trout are never for an instant in the slightest degree interested either in an imitation of the dragonfly or a dead insect impaled on a small hook and carefully cast on to the surface".

On the other hand, according to Ferris, they enjoy this uncanny ability to track and unfailingly intercept even the largest and fastest individuals of our fastest-flying insect group. The dragonfly, observed Ferris, is as much food in the live winged state as it is in the subaqueous larval state. He once examined the stomach contents of a five-pound lake rainbow and found no fewer than 11 mature winged dragonflies. Sorry, George Ferris, but I have yet to be convinced of that track-and-catch-in-mid-air ability of the trout.

Naturally, the nymphs themselves are much more certainly popular with trout, so, forgetting Mottram's and Ferris' experiences, let us consider an item of the trout's diet which Mr A.H. Batten Pooll said formed the principal food of trout in the lakes of the South Island, at least in the summer. But Captain J.S. Phillips would have looked sideways at Mr Batten Pooll for making that observation. Admittedly, the 1920s were early days in the study of aquatic insects in New Zealand, but R.J. Tillyard, an entomologist of some repute, had already said that in certain parts of the country he found dragonfly larvae to be the principal food of trout. "However," commented Captain Phillips dryly, "he doesn't say which parts."

The captain, who was reporting to the Marine Department, in 1929, had found virtually no evidence that trout favoured either larvae or adults in the Wellington district. Even though he speaks of vast numbers of nymphs of a large dragonfly found in the backwaters of the Tukituki, the only evidence of nymphs or adults in the stomachs of any trout examined thus far was limited to one fish taken from a pond close to the Hutt River at Trentham.

Even so, I think we must ignore Captain Phillips' findings for the Wellington district at that time. Ample evidence from so many sources nowadays suggests that the summer angler who fishes lakes and backwaters without suitable imitations of dragonfly larvae is at a disadvantage. Sometimes, as an experience of Ernest Schwiebert's demonstrates, it is not only the summer angler who may miss out. Read Schwiebert's story in *Nymphs* about the day Dick Coffee and he fished the high-country Tarryall Dam in a spring blizzard. Schwiebert had persuaded a bait fisherman there to let him clean a 2lb brown the man had caught, and he'd found dragonfly nymphs in the stomach. Seeking shelter in the station-wagon for a shivering session of fly-tying, he put together some fat muskrat-bodied weighted nymphs to match those from the trout, and went out into the blizzard to try them out. He caught several rainbows throughout the worst of the snow-squalls. He remarks at the end of the story that dragonfly nymphs are large enough to interest even the largest fish and he has taken more really big fish on their imitations than almost any other type except the big stoneflies.

Dragonfly nymphs in New Zealand are no doubt sought by lake trout in similar conditions; at least the lake-bed is where they are all found — all but one, that is — at any time of year. The exception, the largest of them all, our *Uropetala carovei* nymph, larva of the magnificent black-and-yellow-bodied dragonfly with the five-inch wingspan, the one that sweeps up out of nowhere to perch on rod or hand or hat, the *Uropetala carovei* nymph digs itself a burrow in the muddy banks of streams or spring-fed swamps. I have yet to find out of those water-filled burrows, but the entomologists say that as the nymph matures (which takes perhaps five years, would you believe) it burrows deeper, ending up in a chamber which may be 60cm from the mouth of the burrow and a good 25mm in diameter. Now, if that isn't extraordinary enough, just take note of how this lone larva feeds. It climbs up its water-filled tunnel each night and sits in the entrance, *in the open air,* waiting for small insects to cross its path. If they approach within range of the larva's mask (the hinged grab which shoots out from under its jaws and pinions the victim) they can forget about the way home.

You would be quite right to question a mention of *Uropetala carovei* at all, but I just had to remind you of this extraordinary nymph and its life-style. Although it will perhaps never become trout food, it's the only dragonfly nymph that won't, and if that sounds rather Irish, so be it.

All the others can be imitated and used with every prospect of success in still or sluggishly-moving waters. Remember that our other nine species are widely distributed, that their underwater existence usually spans at least two years, and that, in consequence, imitations large and small can be fished in suitable waters throughout the country and all through the season.

Because the nymphs live among the stones and weeds and detritus of the beds of lakes and rivers, they assume the colours of their environments. Dull browns and greens, and mixtures of both, are the safest body-colours to use in imitations. Keith Draper's Brown Dragonfly Nymph pattern, for instance, with its brown chenille body and brown partridge hackle, recommends itself more than another dressing he gives in *Trout Flies in New Zealand*, Bragg's Dragonfly Nymph, which features a fluorescent lime chenille body and a soft grizzle hackle dyed mustard and palmered along the body. Bragg's Dragonfly Kea Nymph is to be preferred.

Despite the insistence of some tiers that imitations of this nymph should be given tails, note that the naturals have no tails. Adding a tail to a dragonfly nymph pattern is as absurd as putting what appear to be horns on what has been called a horn caddis imitation. Even so, absurdities can succeed; the effectiveness at times of the Hamill's Killer, with its black squirrel tail, as a taker of trout seeking dragonfly nymphs, cannot be denied. Nor, for that matter, is the effectiveness of the Muddler Minnow in the same role.

Despite the pattern's long tail, Schwiebert notes that the Muddler is taken by dragonfly-nymph-hunting trout if it is fished slow and deep along the bottom.

The Americans have come fastest and furthest of the fly-dressers with dragonfly-nymph patterns. The variety and intricacy of their patterns is really astonishing. And I do like the candour of Charles Brooks (even though I find the title of the book his candour comes out of rather amusing, *Nymph Fishing for Larger Trout*) when he talks about patterns. He says you don't really need to know what dragonfly and damselfly genera and species are in the lake you're going to fish. If you have a representation of each suborder in three sizes and three colours then you'll be able to find one which will work.

He would want brown, tan, and grey dragonfly nymphs in sizes 4, 6, and 8, on 2x long hooks.

The further one takes researches into trout foods the world over, the more obvious it becomes that, give or take a few millimetres, shapes and sizes of the orders of aquatic insects common to all countries remain the same. Colours differ, but not a great deal, generally speaking, so that what dressing goes down well in Montana will probably go down equally well in Hampshire or Southland.

Simplicity in design and production of proved patterns appeals to most fly-tiers. Couple such simplicity with the advantage of readily-obtainable materials, and the average angler is thoroughly satisfied with that kind of pattern. Because of such considerations, I cannot recommend the quite delightful dragonfly-nymph pattern offered by Whygin Argus in Robert H. Boyle and Dave Whitlock's *The Fly-Tyer's Almanac*. It demands a nymph shape, in felt, cut from an old olive-brown fedora hat made by the English firm of Lock and Co. for Brooks Brothers. The originator of this Old Hat Dragonfly Nymph tells the reader that although dealers in fly-tying materials do not offer these hats for sale they can be found in unattended cloakrooms at almost any Manhattan men's club during the luncheon hour. . .

The collection of such material in New Zealand could be rather expensive unless a group of fly-tiers clubbed together to fly a light-fingered member to Manhattan for a quick raid. That kind of special ingredient did not appeal to Donald Overfield, who, in his book *Fifty Favourite Nymphs*, gave Taff Price's dressing for a dragonfly nymph because the materials are easily obtained and the fly quite straightforward to tie. The pattern would be attractive, except that it embodies three widely-separated stiff goose-feather fibres to form a prominent tail, and doesn't appear bulky enough for a dragonfly imitation.

No, for our purposes, I do believe John Morton's Annie is entirely appropriate. While the materials themselves are easily assembled, however, the 'weaving' technique which imparts such a lifelike look to the body (and to the bodies of other artificials benefiting from a two-tone result) is initially somewhat daunting for the amateur tier. The body shape is first built out from the shank on both sides with pieces of lead wire glued or cemented into place. The lengths of Swannundaze are tied in at the head and brought round the body shape to the end of the shank and fastened there. Looked at from above, the body shape looks like a miniscule snowshoe. Tying-silk and glue should be used to bind and secure the Swannundaze to the lead 'platform'. The body is now dubbed with the rabbit fur and the strands of Swannundaze are now brought forward to tie the first of the series of knots which will make an overbody.

In John's own words: "With the two long ends of Swannundaze (green on the near side and amber on the other as seen from the eye of the hook), tie an overhand knot as though completing the first part of a reef knot, that is, left (green) over right (amber) and then under (amber). Instead of pulling the knot tight on top of the hook, loosen and open the knot, bringing it to the front (eye) of the hook. Keep the amber on top of the hook. The green or lower half of the knot passes over the hook eye and is pushed under the hook, thus "splitting" the knot. Now pull both ends tight, and snug the knot firmly to the rear of the hook shank. The green end should now lie on the far side of the hook and the amber should be on the side nearest you. Now repeat the process, only this time pass the far side (green) over the amber. Again, split the knot, so that the amber lies on top of the hook and the green underneath. Now, tie in along the rest of the hook shank, knot for knot, keeping the sequence of left (green) over right (amber), pull tight, then right (green) over left (amber), each time splitting the knot."

The materials for John Morton's Annie dragonfly-nymph pattern are:
Hook: 10-12 Mustad 9672
Silk: Black
Body: Rabbit fur dyed olive green, and Swannundaze 17 and 19
Wing-case: Brown speckled turkey-feather
Legs: Partridge or speckled mallard, dyed green.

MORTON'S ANNIE DRAGONFLY NYMPH

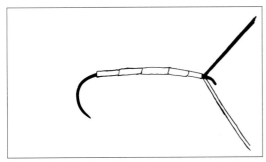

Form the body with lead wire and attach Swannundaze.

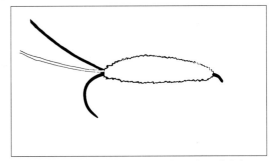

Take Swannundaze back to bend and dub on rabbit's fur.

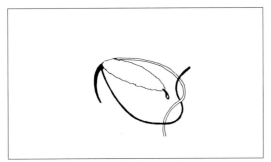

Tie Swannundaze green (left) over amber (right) then under then over.

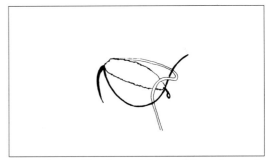

Instead of pulling knot tight, split it and pass it over the eye of the hook. Take snugly to back and pull tight.

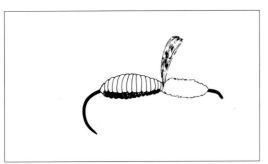

Repeat, keeping green under hook and amber on top, for half length of hook and tie off. Tie in wing case.

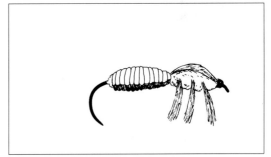

Tie in sets of legs and take wing case to eye. Tie off in normal way.

18
CURSE OF THE FISHERMAN

For a fly so small, the equivalent of an insect which in this country we call the sandfly has made a remarkably profound impression on anglers overseas. Here in New Zealand the only impression the Simuliidae family makes on anyone, angler or not, is the painful one it inflicts when it bites.

We apparently have no patterns for the sandfly, perhaps because no-one has yet bothered to fish so tiny an artificial to our trout. And the reason for that must surely lie in our still largely excellent fishing and our still largely large trout. Why go to the bother of tying sandflies on size 28 hooks when trout will settle for a size 14 sedge?

True, many can't believe that sandflies are legitimate aquatic insects anyway, much less that they like fast water, but aquatic insects they are, and fast water is where most of them are born and bred. Anglers who know these things, and who also know that at times the trout will feed on them to the exclusion of everything else, and that the hundreds of little surface dimples of rising fish include the rings of the largest trout as well as the smallest, have been tying and using Simuliidae imitations in other countries from the earliest days of flyfishing. Fashions change in the gentle art as completely as they change in other fields, and it would seem that right now an upsurge of interest in these tiny naturals of Europe and North America is taking place.

The advance of stream enrichment may well have accounted for the increasing interest in the Simuliidae, just as it has accounted for the growing interest in chironomids. Both families, but especially the chironomids, can tolerate a degree of enrichment unacceptable to some other insects. So, where sandflies and midges abound, flyfishers in Europe and North America are fishing imitations increasingly often. And because their flies are miniscule they

must use gossamer tippets, and correspondingly lighter leaders, lines, and rods. A whole new school of flyfishing has grown up around the stubby little atoms of the troutfisher's insect world.

They don't call them sandflies overseas. In England they call them smuts, reed-smuts, curses, fisherman's curses, blackflies, and sometimes black curses. In the United States they call them riffle-smuts, blackflies, buffalo gnats, and sometimes turkey gnats. No wonder the Latin nomenclature is so important, despite some people's impatience with it. Reference to the Simuliidae, for instance, at once identifies that group of insects anywhere in the world. Talk sandflies in Ootacamund, or buffalo gnats in Gore, and the chances are you won't be understood.

An Englishman who would have known all about sandflies, though, was Dr J.C. Mottram, whose book *Fly-Fishing: Some New Arts and Mysteries*, first published in 1915, recounts some of his New Zealand fishing in 1911 and his solving of the many interesting problems our trout put to him. I like to think that he fished at least one or two of his several smut patterns here. He talks about tying and fishing many artificials in New Zealand, but not specifically the sandfly.

Mottram devotes 14 pages of text, 11 illustrations, and no fewer than eight dressings to the smut in *Fly-Fishing . . .*, and another page and some illustrations, and a further pattern, in a later book, *Thoughts on Angling*, published in 1948 or thereabouts. I am not aware of such an amount of practical information and patterns in any other pair of books. Donald Overfield, the flyfishing historian, who brought the best 50 nymphs together in his 1978 book *Fifty Favourite Nymphs*, 63 years after Mottram's first book, honours one of Mottram's patterns, and a much more modern one of Jacobsen's.

What we don't know about the private life of the sandfly here was revealed for the Simuliidae and closely related species in England many years ago. One of the really extraordinary habits of the males of a species of black curse there described by both Courtney Williams and Goddard involves the securing of a floating dead midge or fragment of plant life, and wrapping it up in the silk that the male secretes. The cunning fellow presents this gift to his lady-love, and while she laboriously unravels the bindings, he makes love to her. Maybe that's why only the females of the smuts, curses, and sandflies bite, perhaps in advance revenge on all and sundry for the dastardly act of the male?

Mating couples often fall on the water, and with the continuing presence of male curses picking up their little presents, trout become especially interested in these paired insects rather than in single ones. On such occasions, which invariably bring most trout, large or small, to the feast at the surface, imagoes on their way from the river-bed to the outer air, attract trout at lower levels. Pupae apparently hatch into adults straight from their pupal cocoons on the bottom and ascend inside a bubble of air, which breaks at the surface to release the fly, quite dry, into the atmosphere.

Fogg gives us a pattern for trout taking the ascending adults. Tied on a size 18 hook, it comprises an underbody of silver wire (to simulate the air in the bubble) ribbed with black tying silk, and a tiny black hen hackle.

Over the years, in fact some say from Charles Cotton himself, who in 1676 gave a dressing for a Black Fly, several patterns for the winged adult have been designed. Some have incorporated pike-scales cut to shape for wings. Halford tells us that a single piece of pike-scale prepared according to Mr MacNee's patent process, cut to shape, and laid flat along the top of the hook, makes the most effective looking wing.

I like Dr Mottram's simple pattern, the one that Overfield recommends in *Fifty Favourite Nymphs*. The cult of the midge, with its somewhat esoteric overtones, may not have spread to New Zealand yet, and precious few flyfishers here may habitually fish patterns tied on hooks I can hardly see, let alone dress, but one of these days we shall need a sandfly, curse, smut, or buffalo gnat pattern. We won't necessarily need it because of a proliferation of Simuliidae but because it may prove to be just what the Doctor ordered for those typically calm, hot, twilights of summer when, as Schwiebert put it, riffle-smut imitations were the secret on several glassy flats along the Brodheads. His patterns were dressed with pale hackle wings and fat little bodies of black polypropylene on size 26 and 28 hooks.

Mottram's pattern is:
Hook: 18
Body: Black floss silk wound in the shape of a tiny bead, tapered off steeply at the aft end, and occupying a little less than half the length of the hook. The rest of the hook is left bare
Hackle: In front of the bead wind on half a turn of the tip of a starling's hackle.

The reference to half a turn of hackle is puzzling, since his illustration shows hackle standing out all round. Perhaps it was his way of saying "as little as possible".

SMUT

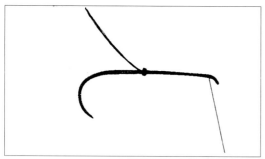

Tie in floss silk for body half way along hook and take thread to eye.

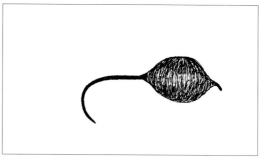

Tie floss for body shape in a bead with a sharp taper at back. Tie off floss.

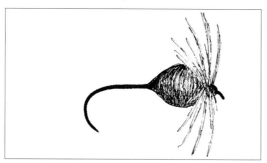

Tie in hackle and take one turn. Tie off and finish.

19
SHRIMPS

Did you ever go shrimping? As a youngster on holiday at the 'seaside' with my parents in those far-off days before World War II in England, I used to paddle across the incoming tide at Worthing to push a shrimp-net over the sands. We would take the catch of ghost-coloured shrimps back in a small seaside bucket to Mrs Pollington's, and cook them for tea while Bertie wound up the gramophone for the hundredth time that day to play his favourite record, "When I Grow Too Old to Dream".

Those shrimps would have been bigger, but not much bigger, than the ghost-coloured shrimps they poured into Lake Taupo in 1912 and 1927 to help feed the trout. Both lots were taken from the Waikato River at Mercer, but presumably the second consignment, of 426,000 shrimps, fared no better than the 110,000 put into the lake 15 years earlier. No doubt the government departments which went to all the trouble of catching and transporting the shrimps, expected them to breed, not knowing that *Paratya curvirostris'* environmental niche apparently limits it to the lower, virtually brackish, waters of rivers and streams entering the sea.

A Mr R. Nielson, who may qualify as the one and only researcher to have taken a genuine interest in the biology of *P. curvirostris* so far in New Zealand, discovered around 1940 that first-stage larvae of the shrimp would die after a few days in fresh water. He could rear them through three or more larval stages in seawater though.

While an abundance of this freshwater prawn, or shrimp, from source to mouth of every river and stream would delight trout and troutfishers throughout the country, we are reluctantly forced to conclude that because of the creature's environmental preferences, the only places where imitations could be fished successfully would be the lower brackish stretches of tidal rivers. In those places, incidentally, bait-fishing may be legal, and although bait has no place in a book of this kind, Keith Draper's mention of freshwater-shrimp baits in his book *Angling in New Zealand* deserves a line or two. Apparently, the method is practised on the Manawatu River, where shrimps proliferate among the willow roots along the banks. Fishermen catch a supply with a net, and boil them lightly in a tin before offering them to the trout on paternoster or ledger tackle.

Now, it is quite possible to tie and fish imitations of our 30mm-long freshwater prawn, and some anglers probably do. Anglers certainly do overseas, where similar crustaceans in places form a significant and substantial trout-food.

But a far more popular, and virtually universal, crustacean, which has qualified for expert fly-tying attention from the earliest times, makes an infinitely more rewarding model. This is the much smaller freshwater shrimp which in some countries goes under the generic name of *Gammarus* but in New Zealand *Paracalliope*. Both genera are of the order Amphipoda, or hoppers, but while shrimps of the genus *Gammarus* are members of the Gammaridae family, our nearest equivalent, *Paracalliope fluviatilis*, belongs not with our own Gammaridae but with the family Eusiridae. This sounds confusing, and it is, but never mind. Generally speaking, the overseas gammarids, and our close relation, resemble the sand-hoppers of our beaches, but the overseas species are somewhat larger, averaging around 10mm, although Schwiebert speaks of *Gammarus* in the United States as growing to 27mm in length. They are all active swimmers and crawlers in and around aquatic vegetation, especially watercress along the edges of slow streams.

Precious little has been published, it appears, about our amphipod shrimps, or even about our larger prawn-like shrimps of brackish water. Admittedly, neither may merit urgent scientific attention, but anglers are surely not the only people interested in these neglected crustaceans? Professor B.J. Marples, as recently as 1962, wrote of our freshwater prawn: "The animal is said to occur in streams throughout the whole of the country." Said to? And anyway, isn't it confined to brackish waters? Since then, as observed by M.A. Chapman and M.H. Lewis in *An Introduction to the Freshwater Crustacea of New Zealand*, published in 1976, "Surprisingly little is known about the biology of these animals [prawns] . . . and the only published information that we are aware of is an abstract of records gathered by R. Nielson in 1940-41. . ."

So New Zealand is not exactly over-supplied with authoritative scientific information about its shrimps. Shame on us.

For those anglers who, like me, would like nothing better than an assurance of 20mm-long *P. fluviatilis* abounding in the weeds of most streams, Captain J.S. Phillips' observations, made in 1929, make tantalising reading: "The commonest and most important [of a host of small crustaceans] is the gammarid *Paracalliope fluviatilis*, which is very minute. *But there is a larger species, found occasionally among watercress; it is about¼in. long and might be worth cultivation. This crustacean has been collected in the upper reaches of the stream at Khandallah, in the Makuri, in the stream flowing through the park at Masterton, and in the Tukituki; it was also noted in a Canterbury stream."* The italics are mine. Is that larger species still about? I think it must be, although no 'popular' literature mentions it.

Captain Phillips was enough of a researcher to know that what he had seen, or what had been reported to him, of a gammarid shrimp ¹/₂in. long, could not be confused with *P. fluviatilis,* which is only a third of its length. Nevertheless, conflicting information confronts the angler seeking truths about shrimps. One authority says shrimps (the prawn type) live in water-weed near the surface of ponds, streams, and rivers. Another says we have no genus *Gammarus,* another that our *Gammarus* is like a small shrimp. But New Zealand hasn't a monopoly on crustacean confusion. Dr J.C. Mottram, who kept and bred shrimps in captivity, writing in England in the mid-1940s in his book *Thoughts on Angling,* said it was evident that although some of the life history of the freshwater shrimp had been elucidated, much still remained to be recorded.

Unquestionably, over the intervening 40 years, much has indeed been recorded of the life and times of *Gammarus* in Britain. Much more has come to light in the United States, however, where both the true freshwater shrimp (or prawn), and the amphipod shrimp, commonly called a scud there, have been given the closest scrutiny, long-term, by biologists, flyfishers, and fly-tiers. Out of that scrutiny has come detailed life-histories and, equally importantly to flyfishers, all manner of patterns realistic and impressionistic. I am filled with admiration for the kind of painstakingly-tied and lifelike representations of the brackish-water shrimp, for instance, as fashioned by Robert H. Boyle in his and Dave Whitlock's *The Fly-tyer's Almanac.* At the same time, let's not forget Courtney Williams' caution over close imitations of the shrimp. Some artificials, he said, look wonderfully lifelike, but don't work. A hackled March Brown, he said, would tempt fish rooting for shrimps among weeds, as would a sunken Claret and Mallard on a 14 hook.

Frank Sawyer's shrimp pattern, tied originally for grayling and then named the Killer Bug by a visiting American who took it home with him and wrought great damage with it in the States, is taken for other natural foods of the trout too. It is well suited to the New Zealand and North American situations as well, for the same reasons that Gary Borger gives for the success of his Red Brown Nymph: the artificial imitates a range of trout foods, including scuds. However, because of the simplicity-itself Sawyer pattern (which a friend of Sawyer's described as a 'miserable concoction of wire and wool') requires a special shade of wool-and-nylon which is hard to come by, I favour a pattern developed by that old master of the nymph, G.E.M. Skues. He tied it on a 16 hook too, which equates with the size of the natural *P. fluviatilis*. Skues is characteristically precise about colours, and clearly they are of considerable importance. But colours here are not necessarily the same as colours there. And colours of one species in one locality there are so often not the colours of the same species in a neighbouring locality.

Skues tied his pattern (on a turned-down-eye Limerick hook) with a pale red hackle dyed olive, a mixture of pale orange and olive seal's fur tied to below the bend of the hook to suggest the curve of the shrimp's back, and ribbed the result with fine gold wire. He hackled the fly palmer-fashion, and cut off all the fibres from the back.

Of course, provided you hit on an appropriate colour for the wool and nylon body, you don't need Sawyer's special shade to tie a Sawyer pattern. So here is a description of the tie. Simply apply two windings of red copper wire and over this base build three layers of the wool-nylon yarn mixture, to finish up with a sausage shape pointed at both ends. Note that the wire, in addition to weighting the bug, does duty as tying-silk as well. That's all there is to it.

Our New Zealand equivalent of the *Gammarus* of Britain and the United States is somewhat of a greyish creature, with dark spots, but obviously you will do well to check the colours of specimens in the waters you fish. Oh, and if you come across any of Captain Phillips' larger species — larger than 4.5mm, that is — let me know, will you?

Hook: 16
Silk: Olive
Body: Mixed pale orange and olive seal's fur
Ribbing: Fine gold wire
Hackle: Pale red hackle dyed olive.

SHRIMP

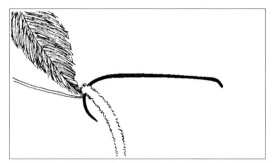

Tie in dubbed thread, hackle and ribbing.

Make body and tie off.

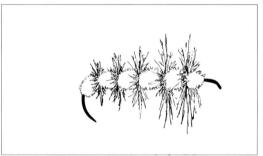

Wind hackle through to eye and follow with ribbing to secure. Tie off.

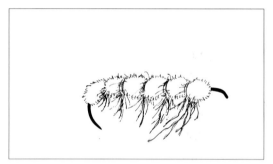

Cut off hackle above body.

20
HAIL, HAIL, THE SNAIL!

Fifteen years ago, the snails in the shallows along the shores of Alex Behrendt's Two Lakes Fishery enjoyed privileges unknown to their distant cousins in New Zealand. No notices warning flyfishers to 'Keep Off the Snails' had ever been erected, but no wading was allowed. Consequently, none of the many snails, or caddis either, for that matter, both so common in the shallows, were trampled underfoot. Behrendt knew just how valuable those snails were to his trout, and thus to himself, proprietor of one of the finest and most meticulously managed private stillwater fisheries in England.

Two Lakes is utterly dissimilar to any stillwater fishery in New Zealand. One day likenesses may develop, forced on us here by gross manifestations of Roderick Haig-Brown's belief that "all pollution is the use of public property for private profit", or by excessive political or fishing pressures. Dramatic changes could also emerge from greater and greater worship of the user-pays principle, or from the indifference of government agencies to the needs of a healthy environment. We ignore the loud and clear messages of overseas freshwater calamities at our peril, and yet we continue to ignore them, and ignore them, and ignore them.

Let us not be too certain that the Two Lakes experience will never be ours. But it is unlikely only if we begin to heed the insistent voices from overseas instead of seeming to take the crassest kind of pride in demonstrating that we're old enough to take that kind of adversity on the chin.

Wading at Two Lakes wasn't prohibited only because of the snails and the caddis. It scared the trout. Boating wasn't allowed, either. Why? So that trout couldn't be pursued or harried in every corner of their home. Shooting-head lines were banned too, because the aim of shooting-head lines is to achieve very long casts, and trout rising to a fly at the end of a very long line are too often merely pricked, or quite often lost. Pricked or lost fish are known to be disinclined to rise to artificial flies thereafter, and thus become a liability. Neutralising such liabilities was achieved by a regulation requiring all landed fish to be killed, whatever their size. The limit was five fish each of .4kg or over, but any smaller fish killed on the way to a limit weren't counted.

If some of the original regulations at Two Lakes have since been revised, be sure that the no-wading restriction remains in force; snails do form a substantial proportion of trout food in some fisheries, and where they populate the shallow edges of well-patronised rivers and lakes, what's the point of trampling them to death? I can remember crushing dozens of little *Potamopyrgus* snails underfoot at Lake Tutira. They seemed to give my thigh-boots a better grip on the slippery stones along the shore. Nowadays, I wouldn't feel easy about repeating that performance. I believe that, even now, the freedom with which we wade in many New Zealand waters adversely affects the food-supply, and thus the trout. I wonder, for instance, how many crayfish and dragonfly nymphs I destroy every time I wade along Whakaipo Bay, here at Lake Taupo. True, no damage I could ever do by wading will have any measurable effect on this enormous (by comparison with Two Lakes) fishery, but I'm only one of thousands.

At least, wading here at the northern end of the lake, I am crushing precious few *Potamopyrgus* snails, if any at all, because for some reason they don't favour this end. And anyway, even though they are apparently the most common of the four species of snails found in the lake, I don't ever recall finding these small dark gastropods in Taupo trout. In trout much further south of the lake, the situation may not have changed greatly since Captain Phillips' day. His official study of trout food in the Wellington province, published in 1929, revealed that two species of *Potamopyrgus* snails present in enormous numbers in the province made up 10 percent of the food taken by the trout he examined.

Snails of the genus *Potamopyrgus* can no doubt be imitated by fly-tiers, and perhaps are, but, especially if you fish stillwaters, lagoons, and backwaters, imitations of larger snails of another type are much to be preferred. This type, the pulmonate type of snail, must occasionally come to the surface to breathe. Once there, it walks upside-down on its water ceiling, so to speak, from which leisurely trout remove it with relish. The other kind of snail, represented by *Potamopyrgus* species, for instance, 'filters' oxygen from the water and therefore has no need to surface. This type, the operculate type, has a bony plate called an operculum with which it seals off its shell whenever the occupant seeks sanctuary or needs to get away from it all once in a while.

Lymnaea stagnalis, one of the pulmonate species that comes to the surface (incidentally, it was specially imported from England as food for trout), will often measure 50mm in length. I haven't yet recovered any that big, not even from Otamangakau trout, but the day could well come when I will; snails up to half that size are commonly found in trout taken from the Big O. The real *escargot* specialists, whose stomachs may be packed with snails, exhibit distended vents, and bellies which, as Roger Fogg puts it, feel crunchy to the touch.

Another pulmonate snail, *Physa acuta*, is also freely taken. More and more often I am catching Taupo trout in which substantial numbers of *P. acuta* are present. The snail grows to around 10mm in length, which to my mind is a manageable and common-sense size to imitate. Undoubtedly, artificials of that size are taken for any one of the pulmonates except those with shells shaped like a ram's horn.

Once more, realism has motivated some fly-tiers and impressionism others. Modern realists favour cork bodies. One clever English pattern for the floating snail, designed by Cliff Henry, receives honourable mention from no less an authority than John Goddard. Tied on up to size 10 hooks, the pattern is basically a squat cone of cork slit down the centre and glued round the hook, and then covered with bronze-green peacock herl stripped of all flue except for a length sufficient to finish up with two or three turns around the cork at its widest diameter. In other words, you end up with a cork cone wrapped almost entirely in stripped brown peacock-herl quill but with a narrow band of bronze-green fibres showing at the 'head'. The whole thing is then covered in clear varnish, presumably to prolong the life of the herl.

Other floating-snail patterns have been developed, notably by Bob Church and D. Barker in England, but we don't seem to have developed any such patterns in New Zealand yet. We do have one time-honoured snail pattern, invented by the well-known Rotorua angler and fly-tier Frank Lord, or Lord's Killer fame, and Tony Orman draws attention in his *Trout and Salmon Sport in New Zealand* to the pattern developed by R.W. Berry of Auckland.

However, despite David Collyer's rejection of the Black and Peacock Spider as a snail pattern, this is the artificial to tie. It can be given a cork underbody to make it float just under the surface, or it can be dressed normally and fished at any depth, as T.C. Ivens intended it should. Moreover, it is yet another portmanteau pattern.

Most people believe that we owe the wonderful B & P Spider to T.C. Ivens, author of *Stillwater Fly Fishing*, but Roger Fogg places its origins much further back, with George Bainbridge in fact, whose book, *The Fly-Fisher's Guide*, appeared in 1816. Bainbridge dressed the pattern to imitate a water-spider.

Now, although it thrills the fly-tier and the fly-tier's intellect to fish a realistic Cliff Henry cork snail to a 'snailing' fish, and catch it, few people would agree that the artificial is well and truly realistic. The same can be said of the B & P Spider dressed as a snail imitation, so, realistic or impressionistic, the B & P Spider is no better or no worse an artificial snail than Henry's creature of cork. But talk of water-spiders and snails at once suggests that this pattern is a non-specific, a portmanteau pattern, and so it is. We don't stop at water-spiders and snails either. Fogg is an enthusiast for the B & P Spider, knowing that, with subtle tying variations, trout will take it for several food forms. Some flyfishers may prefer to know precisely what the trout takes a B & P Spider for. The majority, certainly, feel no qualms about exact identification. So what is undeniably the B & P Spider's considerable advantage over other snail artificials is its sufficiently lifelike impersonation of other foods too, notably beetles and water-spiders but, in Fogg's hands, cased caddis and nymphs as well.

David Collyer, in *Fly-Dressing*, reminds us that Ivens' original dressing incorporated a black rib of tying silk and an underbody of floss silk to bulk out the peacock herl. He assumes that the artificial is meant to simulate a water-spider, but although he suggests a tag of silver tinsel or something similar for his own Brown Spider, to resemble the spider's air-bubble, he omits mention of the tinsel for the B & P Spider. Fogg underlines the importance of that silver tag for the water-spider version, advising tying the pattern plump but only half the length of the shank. The hackle should be a long-fibred one, tied very sparse. He

always fishes the pattern very slowly, to ensure the full play of the long hackle fibres.

But we are chiefly interested in snails, which are dressed differently. The body must be tied very plump. As many as 15 bronze herls twisted together may be needed. A tiny black hen hackle completes the fly. Fewer herls will be needed over a cork or foam underbody, but in any case, because of the delicacy of peacock herl, the material can be strengthened by winding it over a thick layer of wet varnish.

Hook: 8-14
Silk: Brown
Body: Bronze peacock herl only (wet pattern); or over cork or foam underbody (floating version)
Hackle: Tiny black hen.

SNAIL

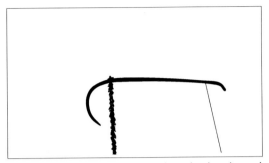

Tie in peacock herl at bend and take thread to eye.

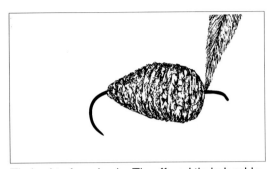

Tie herl to form body. Tie off and tie in hackle. For floating version, tie herls over shaped foam or cork underbody attached to hook.

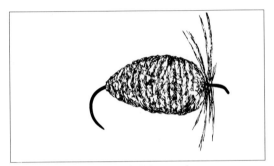

Wind on hackle and finish.

21
THE BOATMAN

When Captain J.S. Phillips checked the stomach contents of a 3lb brown trout from the Lower Selwyn in March, 1929, he could only find water-boatmen — between 300 and 400 of them. Six of nine trout stomachs from Lake Coleridge which he examined later that year and early the next surrendered 486 water-boatmen, of which 237 had been swallowed by a 3lb brown and 212 by a 4 $\frac{1}{4}$lb rainbow.

His exact figures, though, were suspect, and he was the first to admit it. He believed that rod-caught trout frequently void a portion of their stomach contents while on the hook, and that this accounts for the remarkably few adult Ephemeroptera and Diptera found in the stomachs of fish caught during the evening rise, when they have been feeding almost exclusively on such flies.

Although the captain suspected that at least three of the Lake Coleridge fish (including a 12$\frac{1}{2}$lb brown containing only small fragments of digested and unrecognisable matter) had regurgitated stomach-contents, the respectable number of water-boatmen remaining made that food item, at that time, a clear favourite among trout happening on them in Lake Coleridge. I have no doubt whatsoever that, almost 40 years later, the popularity of the water-boatman with trout, wherever the twain shall meet, has not diminished.

Too few analyses of the stomach contents of trout have been published in New Zealand. G.V. Hudson contributed some in 1904, in his book *New Zealand Neuroptera*. A quarter of a century later along comes Captain Phillips with his report to the Marine Department on the food of trout. I hope I am quite wrong, but, apart from a further report by Captain Phillips in 1931, the next collection of analyses appears not to have been made widely known until 1983, when Norman Marsh listed and photographed some in *Trout Stream Insects of New Zealand*. It's one thing to list all the natural foods habitually taken by trout — most flyfishers could surely name the majority without a great deal of thought — but quite another to analyse and publish stomach contents of individual trout taken at certain times in certain waters. Granted, any flyfisher can do that for himself, and should; not only is that small pleasure of considerable assistance on future occasions, it is also a fascinating ingredient of the greater world of flyfishing. But, aside from the angler's own private exploration and records, perhaps detailed analyses, regularly published, covering favourite rivers and lakes around the country, are too much to hope for. But wouldn't it be a help to the visitor to have the local food preferences of trout neatly listed and dated?

No, maybe not: it's really over to the angler, if he's serious enough about his fishing, to carry out his own research. And it's good to do this oneself anyway, not only to identify what the fish are feeding on at a particular time and place, but also to establish what shades of green and brown and other colours are currently fashionable among the various food-forms.

Opinions differ on all kinds of matters piscatorial, and it's no surprise that, in spite of Captain Phillips' findings of 1929, we are told by freshwater biologists in England fairly recently that fewer than one in ten of trout are water-boatman eaters. It really does depend, surely, on what foods are available to trout? Still in England, A. Courtney Williams once stated that since the water-boatman formed a favourite food with trout it was surprising that fly-tiers had paid so little attention to it.

And indeed they haven't. Most surprisingly, the Americans haven't. You can turn up the occasional imitation tied specifically to copy the water-boatman — for instance, Dave Hughes, in his *Handbook of Hatches*, 1987, but unlike tiers elsewhere, notably in England, the Americans seem to prefer relying on a general-purpose pattern — Gary Borger's Red Brown Nymph is a case in point — rather than deliberately attempting a look-alike.

Presumably, then, the water-boatman, and its close relation the backswimmer, isn't considered as important an item of trout-food in the United States as it is in England; or in New Zealand for that matter, where specific dressings are well known. Although one of the New Zealand dressings is actually a time-honoured English pattern, another is a Norman Marsh original.

But what of the water-boatman itself? Does it really deserve a place in the flyfisher's array of imitations? Undoubtedly. Where it is found, and it is found all over the country, so it will be eaten. It's normally a lake-dweller, but it does occur in some rivers and streams. Stillwaters, and the slower reaches of running waters, especially weedy bankside stretches, suit it fine. If not, it can always move on, for this little fellow can fly off to pastures new when it wants.

Our common water-boatman, *Sigara arguta*, is a member of the Hemiptera order of insects, which comprises terrestrial as well as aquatic bugs. Often called a corixid, or lesser water-boatman, to distinguish it from its larger bloodsucking and backswimming relative the backswimmer, *S. arguta* is omnivorous, and lives for most of the time on the bed of its chosen water using its central pair of legs to cling to something solid while it feeds. Like the backswimmer it breathes air. Both make frequent journeys to the surface, rowing themselves along on their long hind legs to replenish their supplies of air. Whereas the water-boatman swims right side up, the backswimmer swims on its back.

Naturally, their need for air exposes them to the attentions of the trout, which will wolf them all day long given the chance. Corixid adults measure only some 6mm in length, but they form a substantial enough tidbit for any hungry trout. Like most insects which spend the greater part of their lives trying not to draw attention to themselves, water-boatmen take on the browns and the greens of the environments in which they live. *S. arguta* favours a mottled dark brown back and paler brown underside, but it would be prudent to dress a mottled dark olive pattern with a light olive underside as an alternative.

A quite distinctive feature of both the water-boatman and the backswimmer is the air bubble they carry. In common with all air bubbles below water, the insects' air supply takes on the silvery look of mercury. The water-boatman stores its bubble between the body and the wings, but in its descent from the surface with a new supply, the body seems entirely outlined in silver.

The other prominent feature of the Corixidae is the long hind pair of legs, fringed with hairs, which are used as oars.

So the contrasting dorsal and ventral colours, the silver gleam of trapped air, and the long legs rowing the insect along, need to be reproduced in artificials. As long ago as 1898, Dr C.E. Walker published just such a pattern. Mottram praised it, but found that the points of starling primaries used for the oars were too stiff, and recommended softer feathers, so that they would move backwards and forwards in the water.

Dr Walker's namesake, Commander C.F. Walker, much later, in his classic book *Lake Flies and Their Imitation*, expressed the same reservation about Dr Walker's otherwise excellent corixid imitation. He said that the oars, or paddles, couldn't be better suggested than by a few fibres of grey-brown partridge breast feather, wound on as an ordinary hackle in the centre of the body. Fibres above and below the hook should be twitched off and the remainder positioned, by dubbing-pressure, at an angle of roughly 60° to the shank on each side. Nowadays, pheasant-tail fibres are often used instead. Hughes, for instance, in a rare American pattern, dresses his artificials with pheasant-tail-fibre paddles.

The ingenuity of one English fly-dresser, David J. Collyer, incidentally solved the problem of some anglers who sought to imitate the water-boatman's downward journeying from the surface. He developed a pattern with a polyethylene body which is fished on a sinking line and a leader at least as long as the depth of the water.

The idea is to cast out as far as possible, let the line sink to the bottom, and then retrieve with long slow pulls with pauses in between. The fly is naturally pulled under, and drifts up again, with each pull and pause.

Not all dressers incorporate a silver look to the body. Some attach oars at the eye of the fly, and some dispense with oars altogether. As Brian Clarke observed, in his book *The Pursuit of Stillwater Trout*, however, "really bad corixa patterns are hard to come by", and whether one uses a lifelike representation or a merely impressionistic pattern, it is difficult to avoid attracting trout to it.

Nevertheless, from the range of reasonably recent patterns, and therefore forgetting the worthy 1898 pattern of Dr C.E. Walker, I'm going to plump for a pattern developed by that great all-round controversial English angler Richard Walker — yet another no-relation namesake of Dr C.E. Walker.

He gives two versions, one with an olive back and one with a brown back. The strip of feather used for the back of the insect is tied in at the tail and left hanging off the back of the hook, shiny side (inside) up. Tie in the tinsel there, take thread to eye, tie in floss silk and wind it up and down to form a substantial body. Bring ribbing tinsel four or five turns up the body and tie in. Bring the feather for the back tightly to the eye and tie in. Separate the two outside fibres of the surplus end of the feather, trim off the middle section close to the silk, bend the two oars back along the body and tie in at an angle of about 30° to the body. Hold the tips together and cut them off to the same length just beyond the bend of the hook.

The dressings are:

Olive-backed corixid
Hook: 12
Silk: Olive
Back: Olive-dyed turkey tail
Rib: Gold wire
Body: White or olive floss.

Brown-backed corixid
Hook: 10
Silk: Light brown (Sherry Spinner)
Back: Cock pheasant centre tail
Rib: Gold wire
Body: White or olive floss.

CORIXA

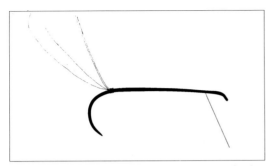

Tie in back feather and ribbing wire and take thread to eye.

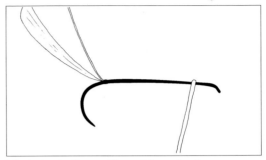

Tie in body floss silk and form body.

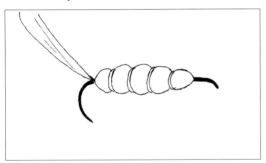

Rib with wire and tie off.

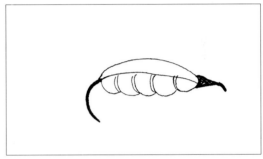

Take back feather over body to eye and tie off.

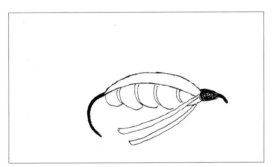

Tie back two outside fibres of back feather for oars.

22
CRAIG'S
CRAYFISH

Fishing the hours of darkness has become a Lake Taupo flyfishing tradition which generates more humour, more frustration, and more trout, than fishing the hours of daylight. Some fishermen consider their night-time fishing the most rewarding of all, and in terms of fish landed, they're right. You only have to fish all day at a shallow stream-mouth, shall we say, and then come back and fish it up to the end of legal fishing time at midnight, to find out whether daylight or darkness brings the greater response from the fish.

Smelt usually move out from the shallows to the safety of deeper water at night, but at the same time bullies and crayfish venture inshore from their deeper daytime quarters. And the trout naturally follow them in. Although smelt may not feature on the trout's after-dark menu, bullies and crayfish — especially crayfish — do. Particularly in shallow waters too, the trout clearly feel a greater sense of security by night than by day. What quite often appears to the daytime angler an exasperatingly barren bay often becomes an exciting battleground pulsing with life by night.

Nowhere is after-dark expectation higher than at the mouths of the several rivers and streams feeding the lake. Among them, the Waitahanui mouth stands supreme. It was once the scene of an angling episode, crucial to this chapter on the crayfish, which I shall come back to later on.

Meanwhile, imagine me, one pleasantly warm and cloudy night on the beach at Wharewaka Point, 3 km north of Waitahanui, fishing not over-confidently below a quarter-moon which unhappily spent more time riding serenely in view than decently hiding its face. Nevertheless, from that seemingly bottomless pit of water on the northern side of the point, I had coaxed a 2.5 kg brown trout an hour earlier. It was nothing to write home about. True, the head was most magnificently savage, but it was a head joined to a body which had seen better days.

One of the interesting things about after-dark fishing at Wharewaka is the surprising frequency of pulls and plucks from crayfish. On nights when trout are elsewhere, those delicate takes keep you on the alert. Perhaps aggression motivates the big crustaceans of Wharewaka Point more compellingly than elsewhere, but they do go for the lure, and sometimes, having captured it, they can't let go.

When the moon next sailed into view I was retrieving the Craig's Night-time (itself a crayfish imitation) up the steep slope of the bottomless pit in front of me. A definite tug registered the interest of some creature down below, so I struck, and a minute later deposited a 150mm crayfish on the beach. He reared unsteadily up at me, letting go the lure, and his eyes blazed red in the light of the torch. I added insult to injury by picking him up, and he shook arms and legs at me wildly until I slid him back into the water.

I don't think crayfish come much bigger than 150mm in Lake Taupo, but large trout will tackle them lovingly whatever their size. No doubt they prefer smaller specimens when they can get them, particularly the soft-shelled ones they catch just after the crustaceans shed their old carapaces. Lake crayfish appear to grow possibly to twice the size of their small-stream cousins, but whether they live in running or still waters they make a favourite food of trout. Judged by the number and variety of pieces of crayfish-jigsaw you find inside some fish, trout must take some time to demolish a hefty hard-shelled specimen. Strangely, I have never yet found a small whole crayfish inside a trout, yet when the youngsters leave home they are apparently only about 25mm long.

Crayfish are distributed widely throughout the country, but not in some South Island lakes, and as they live in every variety of water and are so sought-after by trout, flyfishers who can turn a blind eye on their refusal to look like flies, or even small fish, should carry and fish imitations, especially on after-dark occasions.

Like the shrimp, the crayfish has been almost entirely neglected by biologists in New Zealand. Unless that neglect has been remedied in the past decade, published information of consequence appears to be limited to a 1915 summary of material available up to that year, one or two studies of crayfish in Wellington streams published in 1966 and 1967, and a short general survey, which leans heavily on the same Wellington-streams studies, published in 1976.

Crayfish are found in rivers and streams and in all manner of still waters down to at least 50m. They normally shelter from trout and shags and other predators during the day in burrows or retreats in banks, under stones, in weeds, or in river or lake-bed detritus. They feed at night, coming out of their retreats into shallower waters to eat decaying vegetable or animal matter, or catch what slow-moving organisms they can; snails, for instance (but it was once reported by a Pahiatua angler that he watched a large crayfish attack and kill a passing trout).

When threatened, *Paranephrops* can move rapidly backwards out of harm's way by flapping its tail: hence the knowledgeable fly-tier's invariable custom of dressing lifelike imitations to face the bend of the hook. Such a fly-tier also makes a practice of reversing the hook. Why? To frustrate any tendency on the part of the artificial to catch up on the bottom, where the natural spends its life and where, naturally enough, the imitation should be fished.

In the absence of detailed information, the angler must make do with what slender research resources are available to him, and although the lives and times of crayfish in Wellington streams and Lake Taupo may differ in marked degree, perhaps a kind of statistical average of the two will serve, in the meantime, to typify crayfish elsewhere.

Looked at from above, they are usually a dull brownish-green in colour, resembling the backgrounds in which they are normally found. They cast their shells, or carapaces, several times in their first year, and on fewer and fewer occasions over the succeeding three years, by which time they will have reached sexual maturity. So they are quite long-lived.

It would seem that egg-bearing (berried) females (which, depending on their size, may produce up to 170 eggs, which may take up to four months to hatch) occur between April and December. The first young appear about September, and will probably stay with their mother until December or January, when 25mm long. The eggs are actually carried cemented to the female's abdominal limbs, and when the larvae hatch out they cling among the legs until their third moult, at which stage they leave their travelling home to lead lives of their own.

Immature specimens of the two New Zealand crayfish *Paranephrops planifrons* (the only North Island species) and *Paranephrops zealandicus* are imitated in an extraordinarily lifelike way by a few gifted tiers. I know one keen trout-fishing tier who spent an hour fashioning such a pattern, and then lost it on a rock within ten minutes of christening it. He hasn't tied any more. Excellent imitative patterns have been published in the United States, but apparently none in Britain, where that fine writer and angler Eric Taverner nevertheless believed that trout in Cotton's Dove were extraordinarily fond of crayfish, and that (dare we say it) the trout of the lower Itchen knew the crustacean when they met it.

Here in New Zealand two artificials represent the crayfish, but neither of them would carry off a prize for exact imitation. Both were developed in the 1930s, both have since become Taupo flies by adoption (although one started off in the King Country), and one of them owes a great deal to Fred Fletcher, the then proprietor of Waitahanui Lodge.

Keith Draper and Budge Hintz have delved into the past to tell the stories

of the two crayfish patterns, first Hintz in 1955 in Trout at Taupo, where he recalls the origins of the Craig's Night-time, and then Draper in 1969 and 1971. Draper's 1969 book, *Mr Hundred Per Cent*, discusses the Craig's, and his *Trout Flies in New Zealand* both the Craig's and the Fuzzy Wuzzy, the latter a Fred Fletcher original.

To look at it, you wouldn't think that Fred Fletcher designed the Fuzzy Wuzzy to simulate a crayfish, but then Craig's Night-time is hardly what you would describe as a crayfish look-alike either. The Fuzzy Wuzzy, tied on hooks between sizes 2 and 8, features a red or black chenille or wool body (although other colours are acceptable too, particularly green and orange), a black squirrel tail, and two black hackles, one at the head and the other half-way along the body. A small fly requires only one hackle at the head, a large one three hackles. Draper says that the fly is often erroneously referred to as a Hairy Dog. Originally, it was tied with a large hackle tied palmer-wise along the body. Retrieved in short jerks, the long hackle would draw in against the body and then spread out again.

Craig's Night-time was the invention of a Mr Craig, whose first name was either Eric or Charles, and who hailed from either Auckland or the King Country. So far, then, the facts are somewhat uncertain, but there's no doubt that Mr Craig it was who developed the crayfish pattern bearing his name, and no doubt, either, that the fly introduced the use of pukeko feathers to New Zealand fly-tiers.

Draper's background information about the fly carries no reference to a crayfish, however, but in Budge Hintz's mind and memory the big crustacean of fresh water was the model for Mr Craig's fly. To the best of Hintz's belief, he himself was present when the fly was first fished at Taupo. A few anglers were fishing the Waitahanui rip one bright moonlight night. The most fish were caught by a new arrival from the King Country, Charlie Craig, who was trying out one version of a crayfish fly he tied for his local waters.

Perhaps it doesn't matter all that much at night, but the colour of the Craig's differs substantially from the colour of the natural crayfish. Mr Craig tied a moonlight-night version with a light blue chenille body ribbed with flat silver tinsel and a wing of three broad blue pukeko feathers tied flat along the top. A single jungle-cock eye feather was tied over the top of those to lie flat down the middle. For dark nights, the light blue chenille body was replaced with a pattern featuring a black body. Both dressings embodied a red wool tag.

And that's substantially how the Craig's Night-time is tied today, except that, as might be expected, the jungle-cock is normally omitted by commercial tiers, who customarily dress only the black-bodied version.

Hook: 2-10
Body: Black wool or chenille, ribbed with silver tinsel
Wing: Blue pukeko breast feathers
Tag: Red
Hackle: Black
Topping: One jungle-cock eye laid on top of the blue wings.

CRAIG'S NIGHT-TIME

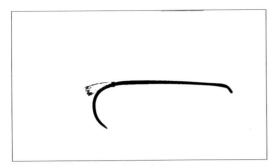

Tie in tag at bend of hook.

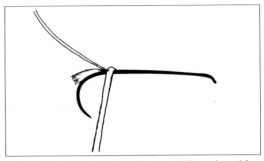

Tie in body wool or chenille and silver tinsel for ribbing.

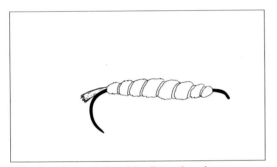

Wind body and rib with silver tinsel.

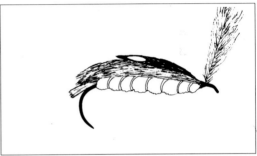

Tie in wing of pukeko breast feathers and jungle feather topping. Tie in hackle.

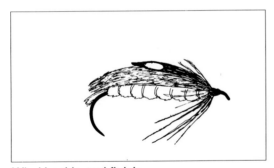

Wind hackle and finish.

23
SPIDERMAN AND
THE BLACK SPIDER

When the trout of W.C. Stewart's beloved border streams were taking winged wet flies just as readily as hackled ones, the great Scots angler prudently fished one, or two, or all, of his three favourite winged wet flies. You see, the large number of trout he was used to catching would eventually tear winged artificials to shreds, but never as quickly as they would demolish the hackled variety. Stewart expected a winged fly to last a day, or even two. When trout were eagerly taking his hackled flies, however, he would have to put on a new one two or three times a day.

Changing flies a dozen times a day, or perhaps more, is no longer a chore, but in Stewart's day it would really have burdened the angler. Men tied flies with their fingers then. They used 'blind' hooks too. Every hand-held hook had first to be furnished with a gut link before fly-tying could begin. And as it was the custom in those days to soak the gut making up links, or casts, for at least 15 minutes before use (because dry gut would fracture), replacing a fly was not exactly the simple operation that eyed hooks and nylon make of it today.

Fighting a way back through misunderstandings and hearsay to innovative fly-tying truths and patterns is sometimes difficult, but not so in Stewart's case because he wrote a book, published in 1857, called *The Practical Angler,* which enshrines for all time the author's opinions, lessons and angling philosophy.

Surprisingly, however, the man is still misunderstood and misquoted. At times he is even dismissed as just another old fuddy-duddy whose teachings have no relevance to present-day techniques.

Even quite well-respected angling writers of our time have misinterpreted Stewart, not realising perhaps that his plain truths are written down for all to see and every now and then republished: no fewer than 15 new editions and reprints appeared between 1857 and 1944, making later mistakes of fact and interpretation hard to understand.

I first tried coming to grips with Stewart at the start of my trout-fishing, and failed. When I rediscovered him 15 years ago I read *The Practical Angler* through three times in as many months.

As I have said somewhere before, the book is an eye-opener. The more you read it, the more you learn. When I first wrote about it I rather ungenerously took P.D. Malloch and W. Earl Hodgson to task for misrepresenting Stewart's quite clear instructions on the subject of spiders and specifically the tying of spiders. Now, having re-read the book once more, and also what I wrote about it in 1974, I am relieved to find that my earlier criticism was well-founded.

But *spiders*, you will say? What on earth have spiders to do with trout flies? We know the story about the flyfisher dropping one of his too realistic artificials in the grass and seeing a spider immediately pounce on it, but really . . .

Spiders, though, are what W.C. Stewart still chiefly remains famous for. Everyone else would call them flies these days, and maybe most of his contemporaries would have called them flies too, but in the districts Stewart fished, and in a good many fly-tying books too, the term 'spider', for a special kind of artificial fly brought so notably to our attention from Scotland, persists. And long may it do so.

Stewart has become famous for three things: his series of spiders, his successful advocacy of upstream wet-fly fishing, and the book he wrote explaining these and other Scots matters piscatorial. One modern-day writer refers to Stewart's northern, wet-fly, soft-hackled flies as being sometimes misleadingly called spiders. But in fact spiders are precisely what Stewart felt the patterns represented. He divided commonly-used artificial flies into two classes. "There is first the winged fly, which alone, properly speaking, merits the appellation; and there is the palmer hackle or spider, by which name we mean to call it, *believing that if it resembles anything in the insect world it is a spider.*" The italics are mine.

A second present-day writer, talking of spider patterns, but for use in reservoirs, considers that one of the best stillwater patterns is the Brown Spider. It will take trout, he says, when the Black and Peacock Spider won't. "Now I come to think of it, perhaps that name 'spider' is the real clue: maybe that really is just what the trout take it for."

Stewart was apparently under no illusion about what the artificial resembled, but he would probably have laughed at the idea of fishing a spider anywhere but in his rapid border streams. After all, you need a good current to tumble the fly along and give seeming life to the soft waving hackles, something you surely can't expect still water to provide, although that wouldn't be as bad as fishing the pattern 'on the drag' downstream, which immediately flattens the waving hackle against the body, destroying all resemblance to an insect?

Strange, isn't it, that Stewart should feel that way about drawing a spider across or against the stream, when swimming-nymph artificials are deliberately dressed that way these days? But not really so strange; one of the puzzling things about Stewart is his seeming ignorance of nymphs. Here's a book on flyfishing northern streams by a down-to-earth Scot, and no mention of nymphs.

Some anglers have since equated Stewart spiders, and the Stewart style of fishing them, with nymphs and nymph fishing. But that is not so. Old G.E.M. Skues believed that the only occasion on which Stewart's spiders could have resembled nymphs was when they were fished downstream with a drag, making the hackle hug the body. In fact, he said that spiders are far more probably suggestive of the subimago caught and tumbled by the stream in the very act of hatching.

If Stewart shared the same opinion he never said so. Not only did he never talk of nymphs, he only fleetingly spoke of natural flies; March browns, the mayfly, the stonefly, the midge, the caddis. And he laughed to scorn any suggestion that any of those creatures except perhaps the mayfly drake needed to be imitated precisely.

Stewart may have scoffed at the advocates of exact imitation, notably those insisting that colours must be faithfully copied, but he was always in deadly earnest on the subject of style. "The great point, then, in fly dressing is to make the artificial fly resemble the natural insect in shape, *and the great characteristic of all river insects is extreme lightness and neatness of form.*" The italics are mine.

In consequence, he dressed his spiders and winged flies the way the naturals were dressed, pointing out that the really practical anglers, such as all those who make their living by fishing, don't put a third of the feathers on their flies that some commercial tiers do.

One of those practical anglers he much admired was James Baillie, the professional fisherman who first introduced him to the Black Spider, "made of the small feather of the cock starling, dressed with brown silk . . . upon the whole the most killing imitation we know". Two other spiders, the Red Spider and the Dun Spider, and three winged flies, made up the half-dozen patterns that Stewart considered indispensable. But the spiders were his favourites, and the Black Spider was the one he liked best.

When tying them, remember that they must be tied 'buzz', that is, hackled in this case the length of the body. I say "in this case" because that is how Stewart dressed them, and although several tiers of the present day restrict buzz hackling to one third or so of the body length, there's no point in tying Stewart spiders any other way than originally described.

Like most north country flies, the bodies are short, only about half the length of the hook. They are very slim. The hackle should be the same length of the hook and tied at right angles to the shank for full mobility. Obviously, soft hackles are essential, but though Stewart preferred hen hackles he did use feathers from a cock starling in winter plumage for his Black Spiders because they have a rich glossy black which no other feathers possess.

Stewart's way of tying a spider is quite simple. You tie in the brown tying silk (for the Black Spider) at a point half-way along the shank, take it in tight turns to the eye, form a head, tie in the black feather with stalk facing the rear, cut off the waste end, roll the feather round and round the thread and wind it down to where you started, tie it down and trim off the end. Either during wrapping, or after, it may be necessary to free enough hackle fibres, with a needle, to represent the legs and wings of an insect struggling to hatch. But don't make the artificial too bushy. Stewart felt that the line drawing of a spider in his own book illustrated too bushy a dressing. But, as he said, the trout's teeth would otherwise tear the fibres away too fast. "After capturing a dozen trout it will be spare enough."

Hook: 12 - 16
Body: Brown tying silk
Hackle: Black, preferably cock starling.

SPIDER

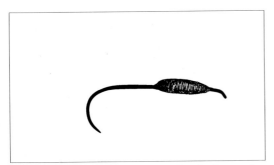

Starting from halfway along shank, form slim body with turns of slik.

Form a head and tie in a black hackle with fibres the length of the hook.

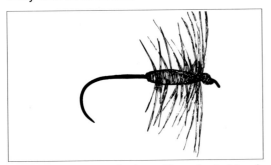

Roll feather around tying silk and wind back to starting point. Tie off and trim waste. Use dubbing needle to free hackles.

24
PYRONOTA FESTIVA

Summer was a very long time a-coming in. Low cloud and clammy winds poured across the last half of December. Suddenly, the first day of the new year dawned bright and beautiful and faintly breezy, and I took the big camera out to Whakamoenga Point to photograph the Tongariro National Park mountains, still deep in snow, beyond Lake Taupo's southern shore.

If I had stayed some hours I might have finished up with some good pictures, but after I had been waiting an hour, green beetles were still blundering around in front of the camera, plainly wanting to share immortality with the mountains. I gave up. I did take some pictures, but they all have green *Pyronota festiva* blobs on.

Some years are bigger green-beetle years than others. It's not often that the young leaves on our big silver birch attract the beetles, but when they do, the insects drip from every branch. Sparrows and starlings fly purposefully straight at the leafy twigs and then swoop down to the ground for the green-beetle bounty they have dislodged. On some days in a good year, when literally millions of green beetles will be about, great slicks of them form on the lake, and ducks and trout endlessly gobble them up. When the weather changes and a big southerly blows, the waves pile mounds of corpses on exposed shorelines.

A visiting angler once wrote that the green beetle, or manuka beetle, was the most famous of all New Zealand trout flies. It is arguable what he meant by that, but our own Captain Phillips considered that although beetles green and beetles brown are of some value as trout food, their season is a short one. Hudson, checking the contents of 60 trout stomachs, listed only 44 green beetles among the 6,094 insects he identified. Only five of the 60 fish had ingested green beetles, and of the five two contained one each, two 15 each, and one 12. That was a pretty poor showing really.

In years when large numbers of the beetle are flying you can catch trout full of them. The greatest number I have ever counted in one fish was 271, a figure which would have lifted Hudson's eyebrows right off his head.

Such a proliferation of green beetles doesn't do a lot for the angler's confidence. He puts an imitation out among hundreds floating on a stillwater bay, and wonders if a trout will ever notice it. Far better to fish running water in green beetle time, particularly if you can spot your trout. Even if lake fish do seem to be sipping down quite a few greenbacks and might indeed get around to yours, the running-water situation has nothing of the lottery about it whatsoever; if fish are taking beetles they will be rising for them in a set place or on a set beat. Your imitation, placed ahead of them, stands a much better chance than on a lake of being taken.

Someone has suggested increasing the interest of river trout by beating beetle-bearing streamside branches upriver of where you want to fish. If you must catch fish for the pot, that's a certain way to do it, provided trout are taking the naturals and provided your artificial is a convincing copy. Otherwise, again with a good imitation, you can always persuade the trout that a beetle feast is upon them by simply working the George La Branche trick; casting so carefully and frequently as to induce the fish into believing a hatch is under way.

I guess if I badly wanted fish (but whatever for; who starves without trout?) I might knock a few upstream branches, but to me groundbaiting and flyfishing just don't go together. Some guides don't think so, naturally enough, I suppose. I know a couple who cheerfully catch cicadas at Lake Otamangakau and throw them out as groundbait for their clients. I know a couple of highly successful flyfishers at the same lake who used to seed particular spots with hundreds of chironomid egg-pouches and larvae, but I'm not going to tell you how they did it. To me, groundbaiting reached its most repugnant level, and troutfishing its sorriest state, in the hands of two or three Tongariro baitfishers who stripped a hen fish of her eggs, threw them in at the head of a rapid, and then fished their trout-egg imitations, Glo-bugs, into the pool below, taking fish after fish in the process.

Strangely, though, perhaps because the book in which it is set was written long ago, and so evocatively, the groundbaiting story Romilly Fedden tells in Golden Days brings only a tolerant smile whenever I read it. If you know the book you will remember how Jean Pierre, Fedden's Breton friend, created a hatch of mayflies and how the hour that followed more than retrieved a hot and irritating summer's day.

In years of plentiful supply, trout throughout the country put on post-spawning condition more rapidly than in leaner years. George Ferris said quite emphatically that the green beetle is responsible for the trout's recovery after

spawning. Incidentally, his solution of the problem posed by attracting green-beetling fish to his imitation among hundreds of naturals on the water was to use something quite different . . .

But it's so satisfying to tie patterns resembling the naturals, and then catch fish on them. Green beetles can be copied fairly easily, using a green back of peacock herl or raffia over a plump little body of light reddish-brown fur and a turn of reddish-brown hackle. But because beetles in the surface film are just as likely to float right way up as upside down, you don't need green backs anyway (though I must say that the two-tone imitations look a lot better to me than plain brown ones). On the other hand, and if you don't tie your own flies or have somehow left all your Green Beetles at home, you can always try a Red Palmer or a Coch y Bonddu, particularly the latter. Don't ever, from November through to the end of January, be without a suitable imitation. Unless the great green beetle carnival is well and truly over, you never know when you'll need an artificial or two.

This is Norman Marsh's dressing:
Hook: 12-16
Thread: Brown
Body: Synthetic brown yarn
Wing case: Peacock eye herl (iridescent green).

GREEN BEETLE

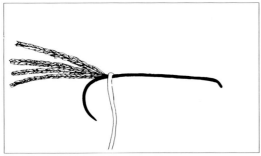

Tie in peacock herls for wing case and body yarn at bend.

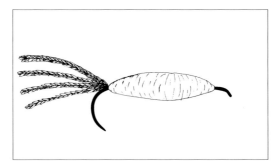

Form body.

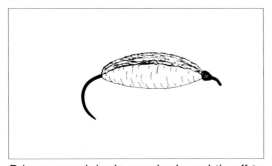

Bring peacock herls over body and tie off to form wing case.

25
LITTLE MICE
BY NIGHT

Francis Francis told us in his *A Book on Angling* in 1867 that rats and mice and small birds make good bait for pike. The first two, he says, make a good bait stuffed with sufficient lead to make them swim properly, and one good hook sticking out of the after part of the belly. "Failing in procuring the skins," he writes, "a tolerable imitation of a water-rat can be made from a bit of the skin of a cow's tail."

I wonder whether a certain old Indian Army major of Turangi, who plainly regarded the big browns of the Tongariro as so many pike, ever experimented with a bit of the skin of a cow's tail? But perhaps quite enough livebaits came his way: he used to pay the local Maori children so much a head for live field mice. According to Budge Hintz, who recounts the story of the major in *Trout at Taupo*, the old chap, in his declining years, considered it his principal mission in life to rid the river of its giant browns, which he said were cannibals and should be destroyed for the benefit of the fishery.

Knowing the considerable agility and speed of wild field mice, I just can't understand how the major extracted his livebaits from the matchboxes in which we are told he took his captives after dark to the river (or ever got them into the boxes in the first place), and then bound them with strong silk to a large hook before floating them down over deep water along overgrown banks.

Other stories of dry-mouse fishing at Taupo and elsewhere in New Zealand persuade me into the belief that the easiest way to a trophy brown trout is after dark with a plump *Mus musculus* imitation. I have not so far succumbed to this mammal-fishing technique, but I just might when the disdainful heavyweights of certain Taupo waters have been even more disdainful than usual by day. They will be encouraged to drop their guard and come hugely at little mice by night. Although night-fishing is no longer one of my weaknesses, the prospect of big browns is. Still, I would much rather bring one to a size 14 Pheasant Tail Nymph, say, by day, as I did close to the Delta one early summer morning along the Tongariro. The fish was no more than 4kg, and it lay tucked down behind a willow tangle, and out in the river to its left lay an old willow stump. The fourth pattern I offered at last switched on that small Tongariro giant. It took the nymph, shook its head disbelievingly, and fled to the willow stump. I knew it would.

One of the advantages of a surprise attack after dark, whatever the lure, is the greater strength of the leader you can use. That's certainly one of the attractions of mouse-fishing, or any other large-lure fishing by night. If you have done your homework and know that the place you are fishing is the home of a big brown trout, the assurance of a stout leader is decidedly comforting. Even so, and especially in the case of a mouse, which must be fished on the surface with drag the whole time, and thus on a taut line, a sudden strike from a large brown is usually very strong and very unnerving.

It's true that reproducing every little physical feature of the mouse is quite unnecessary, but George Leonard Herter felt that legs were really essential. The revised sixteenth edition of his no-nonsense *Professional Fly Tying, Spinning, and Tackle Making*, first published 15 years previously, in 1941, says that probably the most important feature of a hair-bodied mouse, insofar as fish are concerned, is legs. Most people forget them, he says accusingly. He recommends cutting them in pairs from either leather or sheet rubber. A tail can be made from buckskin.

As with the imitation of big terrestrial insects, which also need to float, buoyancy for the mouse is usually achieved with deer hair. Both Herter's and Jorgensen's patterns are constructed of this material, which is clipped to mouse shape. Herter advocates a degree of realism which Jorgensen appears not to bother with. Herter's mouse arms and legs are equipped with definite hands and feet. "Give the mouse plenty of whiskers," he urges. Cut ears from the hair as you go along, or glue little leather ones in later. Tie a bunch of hairs in front of the whiskers and trim it into a nose. Eyes can be painted on, burned in with a red-hot needle, or simulated with commercial glass eyes on wire stems.

By comparison, Jorgensen's clipped deer-hair mouse, a pattern highly recommended in Charles Brooks' *The Trout and the Stream*, only vaguely caricatures the natural. Jack Gartside's imitation, the one included in the second volume of Jack Dennis' *Western Trout Fly Tying Manual*, looks even less like a mouse: it's merely a series of soft grey pheasant under-plumes wound along the hook and finished off with a partridge-hackle collar.

After-dark trout can easily be deceived with imitation mice fashioned from cork or plastic foam too, but the artificials hardly qualify as examples of the fly-tier's art. No matter — the mouse is a legitimate food. On the one hand, using deer-hair, it can be represented with imitations which call for considerable skill and artistry. On the other hand, using solid materials, construction of an

impressionistic mouse becomes easy. Robert Sloane's imitation is ridiculously simple. More correctly it was Robert Sloane's father's imitation, handed down from English north-country fishermen. You take a piece of wine cork, cut a slit along it for the hook shank, and glue and bind the thing in position. "Naturally," says Robert Sloane in his book *The Truth About Trout*, "the permutations and combinations of shape and colour are endless . . ."

Whether tied with hackles, deer-hair, cork, or plastic foam, the imitation needs to sit level on the water, so the underside should be finished flat. Shape the front so that when retrieved at mouse dog-paddle speed across the surface, the artificial creates a substantial ripple.

I can't talk from mouse-fishing experience, but I feel that although legs may give greater realism to an imitation, the feature that really deserves inclusion is the tail. And if you fish such patterns only after dark, it's unlikely that ears and eyes and whiskers are all that important. Sorry about that, Mr Herter. Nevertheless, even though darkness may require us to fish nothing more detailed than a mouse silhouette, complete with tail, most would prefer the artistry of deer-hair construction, and would leave it to tiers like John Morton to show what can be achieved. Here is his pattern:

Hook: Size 4 or 6
Silk: Black
Body: White tail deer hair
Tail: Squirrel tail.

MOUSE

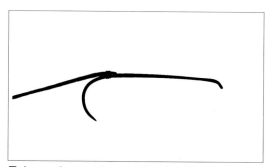

Take a clump of squirrel hair. Glue its entire length and tie to bare hook at bend, using minimum number of turns.

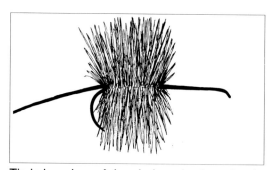

Tie in bunches of deer hair and spin on hook. When hook is half covered, lay hook in vice and push clumps of hair towards bend to pack tightly.

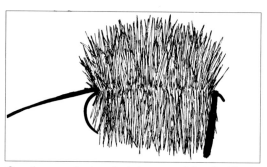

Continue spinning hair to eye of hook. Tie in bunch of squirrel hair whiskers in one clump and keep together at this stage with glue.

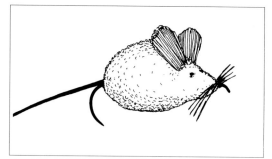

Shape deer hair to desired final shape, remembering to leave enough for ears. Separate squirrel hairs to make whiskers. When tied off, hold in steam to lift any hairs missed when shaping and trim.

A LIST OF THE BOOKS CONSULTED

Allen, K. Radway. *The Horokiwi Stream.* New Zealand Marine Department, Wellington, 1951.

Almy, Gerald. *Tying and Fishing Terrestrials.* Stackpole Books, Harrisburg, 1978.

Arbona, Fred L., Jr. *Mayflies, The Angler, and The Trout.* Winchester Press, Tulsa, 1980.

Atherton, John. *The Fly and the Fish.* Freshet Press, New York, 1971.

Bark, Conrad Voss. *The Encyclopaedia of Fly Fishing.* Batsford, London, 1986.

Bernard, J. *Fly-Dressing.* Jenkins, London, 1932

Berners, Dame Juliana (attrib.) *Treatise of Fishing With an Angle.* As reproduced in John McDonald's *Quill Gordon,* Knopf, New York, 1972.

Best, Thomas. *The Art of Angling.* Crosby & Co., London, 1814.

Borger, A. *Nymphing: A Basic Book.* Stackpole Books, Harrisburg, 1979.

Bowlker, Richard and Charles. *The Art of Angling . . .* M. Swinney, Birmingham, 1788.

Boyle, Robert H. and Whitlock, Dave. *The Fly-Tyer's Almanac.* Crown Publishers, New York, 1975.

Brooks, Charles E. *Nymph Fishing For Larger Trout.* Crown Publishers, New York, 1976.

Burke, Edgar. *American Dry Flies and How to Tie Them.* The Anglers' Club of New York, New York, 1931.

Caucci, Al. and Nastasi, Bob. *Hatches.* Comparahatch, New York, 1975.

Chapman, M.A. and Lewis, M.H. *An Introduction to the Freshwater Crustacea of New Zealand.* Collins, Auckland, 1976.

Chetham, James. *The Angler's Vade-Mecum.* William Battersby, London, 1700.

Clarke, Brian. *The Pursuit of Stillwater Trout.* A. and C. Black, London, 1979.

Clarke, Brian, and Goddard, John. *The Trout and the Fly.* Benn, London, 1980.

Collyer, David J. *Fly-Dressing.* David and Charles, North Pomfret, 1980.

Collyer, David J. *Fly-Dressing II.* David and Charles, Newton Abbot, 1981.

Combs, Trey. *Steelhead Fly Fishing and Flies.* Salmon Trout Steelheader, Portland, 1976.

Cradock, Lieut.-Col. Montagu, C.B. *Sport in New Zealand*. Anthony Treherne, London 1904.

Dennis, Jack. *Western Trout Fly Tying Manual, Vol. I*. Snake River Books, Jackson Hole, Wyoming, 1974.

Dennis, Jack. *Western Trout Fly Tying Manual, Vol. II*. Snake River Books, Jackson Hole, Wyoming, 1980.

Dewar, George A.B. *The Book of the Dry Fly*. A. and C. Black, London, 1910.

Dickinson, P. *Field Notes for the Freshwater Naturalist*. Dominion Museum, Wellington, 1951.

Dickinson, R. *Rising Fish*. Whitcombe and Tombs, Christchurch, 1956.

Draper, Keith. *Angling in New Zealand*. A.H. & A.W. Reed, Wellington, 1978.

Draper, Keith. *Mr Hundred Per Cent: Fred Fletcher's Taupo Tales*. A.H. & A.W. Reed, Wellington, 1969.

Draper, Keith. *Nymphs for All Seasons*. Tackle House, Taupo, 1973.

Draper, Keith. *Trout Flies in New Zealand*. A.H. & A.W. Reed, Wellington, 1971.

Dunne, J.W. *Sunshine and the Dry Fly*. A. and C. Black, London, 1924.

Edmonds, Harfield H. and Lee, Norman N. *Brook and River Trouting*. Bradford, n.d. (1916).

Elder, Frank, *The Book of the Hackle*. Scottish Academic Press, Edinburgh, 1979.

Ephemera. *A Handbook of Angling*. Longman, Brown . . . , London, 1848.

Fedden, Romilly. *Golden Days*. A. & C. Black, London, 1919.

Ferris, George. *Fly Fishing in New Zealand*. Heinemann, Melbourne, 1954.

Ferris, George. *The Trout Are Rising*. Heinemann, London, 1964.

Flick, Art, ed. *Art Flick's Master Fly-Tying Guide*. Crown Publishers, New York, 1977.

Flick, Art. *Art Flick's Streamside Guide*. Crown Publishers, New York, 1969.

Fogg, W.S. Roger. *The Art of the Wet Fly*. A. and C. Black, London, 1979.

Forsyth, D.J. and Howard-Williams, C. *Lake Taupo*. Department of Scientific and Industrial Research, Wellington, 1983.

Fox, Charles K. *Rising Trout*. Hawthorn Books, New York, 1978.

Francis, Austin M. *Catskill Rivers*. Nick Lyons Books, New York, 1983.

Francis, Francis. *A Book on Angling*. Herbert Jenkins, London, 1920.

Fysh, Sir Hudson. *Round the Bend in the Stream*. Angus and Robertson, Sydney, 1968.

Gerlach, Rex. *Creative Fly Tying and Fly Fishing*. Stoeger, South Hackensack, 1978.

Gillett, Alex, and Perry, Jane. *Taupo Fishing Diary*. Hodder and Stoughton, Auckland, 1981.

Ginrich, Arnold. *The Fishing in Print*. Winchester Press, New York, 1974.

Gingrich, Arnold. *The Joys of Trout*. Crown Publishers, New York, 1973.

Gingrich, Arnold. *The Well-Tempered Angler*. Knopf, New York, 1966.

Goddard, John. *Stillwater Flies: How and When to Fish them*. Benn, London, 1982.

Goddard, John. *The Super Flies of Still Water*. Benn, London, 1977.

Goddard, John. *Trout Fly Recognition*. A. and C. Black, London, 1966.

Grey of Falloden, Viscount. *Fly Fishing*. Dent, London, 1947.

Griffiths, F.A.D. *The Lure of Fly-Tying*. Murray, Ultimo, 1978.

Grove, Alvin R., Jr. *The Lure and Lore of Trout Fishing*. Freshet Press, New York, 1971.

Halford, F.M. *Dry-Fly Fishing in Theory and Practice*. Sampson Low. . . , London, 1889.

Hamilton, G.D. *Trout-Fishing and Sport in Maoriland*. Government Printer, 1904.

Harder, John. *Index of Orvis Fly Patterns*. Orvis, Vermont, 1978.

Harding, E.W. *The Flyfisher and the Trout's Point of View*. Seeley Service, London, 1931.

Harris, J.R. *An Angler's Entomology*. Collins, London, 1952.

Henderson, William. *My Life as an Angler*. Satchell, Peyton, London, 1879.

Herter, George Leonard. *Professional Fly Tying, Spinning, and Tackle Making Manual and Manufacturers' Guide*. Herter's, Minnesota, 1966.

Hewitt, Edward R. *A Trout and Salmon Fisherman for Seventy-Five Years*. Scribner's, New York, 1950.

Hickling, Harold. *Freshwater Admiral*. A.H. & A.W. Reed, Wellington, 1960.

Hills, John Waller. *A History of Fly Fishing For Trout*. Phillip Alan, London, 1921.

Hills, John Waller. *River Keeper*. Bles, London, 1934.

Hintz, O.S. *Fisherman's Paradise.* Reinhardt, London, 1975.

Hintz, O.S. *Trout at Taupo.* Reinhardt, London, 1955.

Hobbs, G.B. *Fisherman's Country: Days in New Zealand.* Bles, London, 1955.

Hudson, G.V. *An Elementary Manual of New Zealand Entomology.* West, Newman, London, 1892.

Hudson, G.V. *Fragments of New Zealand Entomology.* Ferguson and Osborn, Wellington, n.d. (1950?).

Hudson, G.V. *New Zealand Neuroptera.* West, Newman, London, 1904.

Hughes, Dave. *Handbook of Hatches.* Stackpole Books, Harrisburg, 1987.

Imms, A.D. *Insect Natural History.* Collins, London, 1947.

Jacques, David. *The Development of Modern Stillwater Fishing.* A. and C. Black, London, 1974.

Jackson, W.S. *Notes of a Fly Fisher . . .* Fishing Gazette, London, 1933.

Jacques, David. *Fisherman's Fly.* A. and C. Black, London, 1965.

Jennings, Preston. *A Book of Trout Flies.* Crown Publishers, New York, 1970.

Jolly, V.H. and Brown, J.M.A. *New Zealand Lakes.* Auckland University Press, Auckland, 1975.

Jorgensen, Poul. *Modern Trout Flies and How to Tie Them.* Nick Lyons Books, New York, 1979.

Kaufmann, Randall. *American Nymph Fly Tying Manual.* Amato, Portland, 1977.

Kelly, Greg. *The Flies in My Hat.* Hodder and Stoughton, London, 1967.

Kite, Oliver. *Nymph Fishing in Practice.* Jenkins, London, 1963.

LaFontaine, Gary. Caddisflies. Winchester Press, New York, 1981.

Lapsley, Peter. *The Bankside Book of Stillwater Trout Flies.* A. and C. Black, London, 1978.

Lawrie, W.H. *A Reference Book of English Trout Flies.* Pelham Books, London, 1967.

Leonard, J. Edson. *Flies . . . A Dictionary of 2200 Patterns.* Barnes, New York, 1950.

Lively, Chauncy. *Chauncy Lively's Flybox: A Portfolio of Modern Trout Flies.* Stackpole Books, Harrisburg, 1980.

Macan, T.T. and Worthington, E.B. *Life in Lakes and Rivers.* Collins, London, 1951.

McCausland, M.E. *Fly Fishing in Australia and New Zealand.* Lothian, Melbourne, 1949.

McDonald, John, ed. *The Complete Fly Fisherman: The Notes and Letters of Theodore Gordon.* Scribner's, New York, 1947.

McDonald, John. *Quill Gordon.* Knopf, New York, 1972.

McDowall, Dr Bob. *Trout in New Zealand Waters.* Wetland Press, Wellington, 1984.

McDowall, R.M. *New Zealand Freshwater Fishes._*Heinemann, Auckland, 1978.

McDowell, Hugh. *New Zealand Fly Tying.* A.H. and A.W. Reed, 1984.

Mannering, G.E. *Eighty Years in New Zealand.* Simpson and Williams, Christchurch, 1943.

Marinaro, Vincent, C. *In The Ring of the Rise.* Crown Publishers, New York, 1976.

Marinaro, Vincent, C. *A Modern Dry-Fly Code.* Crown Publishers, New York, 1970.

Marples, B.J. *An Introduction to Freshwater Life in New Zealand.* Whitcombe and Tombs, Christchurch, 1962.

Marsh, Norman. *Trout Stream Insects of New Zealand.* Millwood Press, Wellington, 1983.

Migel, J. Michael. *The Masters on the Dry Fly.* Lippincott, Philadelphia, 1977.

Migel, J. Michael, and Wright, Leonard M., Jr. *The Masters on the Nymph.* Nick Lyons Books, New York, 1979.

Miller, David. *Common Insects in New Zealand.* Reed, Wellington, 1984.

Mosely, Martin E. and Kimmins, D.E. *The Trichoptera of Australia and New Zealand.* British Museum, London, 1953.

Mottram, J.C. *Fly-Fishing: Some New Arts and Mysteries.* Field Press, London, n.d. (1921).

Mottram, J.C. *Thoughts on Angling.* Jenkins, London, n.d.

Murphy, Brian, comp. *The Angler's Companion.* Paddington, New York, 1978.

Nelson, William. *Fishing in Eden.* Witherby, London, 1922.

Orman, Tony, *The Sport in Fishing.* A.H. and A.W. Reed, Wellington, 1979.

Orman, Tony, comp. *Trout and Salmon Sport in New Zealand.* Reed, Wellington, 1980.

Orman, Tony. *Trout with Nymph.* Collins, Auckland, 1983.

Overfield, T. Donald. *Famous Flies and Their Originators*. Adam and Charles Black, London, 1972.

Overfield, T. Donald. *Fifty Favourite Nymphs*. Benn, London, 1978.

Overfield, T. Donald. *G.E.M. Skues: The Way of a Man with a Trout*. Benn, London, 1977.

Parsons, John. *A Fisherman's Year*. Collins, Auckland, 1974.

Parsons, John. *Parsons' Glory*. Collins, Auckland, 1976.

Parsons, John. *A Taupo Season*. Collins, Auckland, 1979

Pendergrast, J.G. and Cowley, D.R. *An Introduction to New Zealand Freshwater Insects*. Collins, Auckland, 1966.

Pennell, H. Cholmondeley. *Fishing Gossip*. A. and C. Black, Edinburgh, 1866.

Phillips, J.S. *A Report on the Food of Trout*. New Zealand Marine Department, Wellington, 1929.

Pickard, F.W. *Trout Fishing in New Zealand in Wartime*. Putnam's, New York, 1940.

Pooll, A.H. Batten. *Some Globe-trottings With a Rod* . Spottiswoode, Ballantyne, London, 1937.

Pritt, T.E. *North-Country Flies*. Sampson Low. . ., London, 1886.

Ransome, Arthur. *Rod and Line*. Cape, London, 1929.

Raymond, Steve. *Kamloops*. Frank Amato, Portland, 1980.

Rennie, James. *Alphabet of Angling*. William Orr, London, 1833.

Ritz, Charles. *A Fly Fisher's Life*. Reinhardt, London, 1972.

Roberts, John. *The New Illustrated Dictionary of Trout Flies*. Allen and Unwin, London, 1986.

Ronalds, Alfred. *The Fly-Fisher's Entomology*. Jenkins, London, 1921.

Rosborough, E.H. "Polly". *Tying and Fishing the Fuzzy Nymphs*. Stackpole Books, Harrisburg, 1978.

Salter, T.F. *The Angler's Guide* . . . Sherwood & Co., London, 1825.

Sawyer, Frank. *Nymphs and the Trout*. A. & C. Black, London, 1981.

Schwiebert, Ernest G., Jr. *Matching the Hatch*. Macmillan, New York, 1955.

Schwiebert, Ernest. *Nymphs*. Winchester, 1973.

Schwiebert, Ernest. *Trout*, Deutsch, London, 1979.

Scotcher, George. *The Fly Fisher's Legacy.* Honey Dun Press, London, 1974.

Senior, William. *Travel and Trout in the Antipodes.* Chatto and Windus, London, 1880.

Shaw, D.J., Fletcher, M., and Gibbs, E.J. *Taupo — A Treasury of Trout.* New Zealand Wildlife Service and the Central North Island Wildlife Conservancy Council, Taupo, 1985.

Skues, G.E.M. *Minor Tactics of the Chalk Streams.* A. and C. Black, London, 1950.

Skues, G.E.M. *Nymph Fishing for Chalk Stream Trout.* A. and C. Black, London, 1939.

Skues, G.E.M. *Side-Lines, Side-Lights & Reflections.* Seeley Service, London, 1932.

Skues, G.E.M. *The Way of a Trout with a Fly.* A. and C. Black, London, 1921.

Sloane, Robert D. *The Truth About Trout.* Tas-Trout Publications, Tasmania, 1983.

Solomon, Larry, and Leiser, Eric. *The Caddis and the Angler.* Stackpole Books, Harrisburg, 1977.

Southland Acclimatisation Society. *Trout Fishing in Southland, New Zealand.* Southland Acclimatisation Society, 1978.

Spackman, W.H. *Trout in New Zealand: Where to Go and How to Catch Them.* Government Printer, Wellington, 1892.

Sparse Grey Hackle. *Fishless Days, Angling Nights.* Crown Publishers, New York, 1971.

Stewart, Dick. *Universal Fly Tying Guide.* Stephen Greene Press, Massachusetts, 1979.

Stewart, Douglas. *The Seven Rivers.* Angus and Robertson, Sydney, 1966.

Stewart, W.C. *The Practical Angler.* A. and C. Black, London, 1944.

Stokell, G. *Fresh Water Fishes of New Zealand.* Simpson and Williams, Christchurch, 1955.

Sturgis, William Bayard. *Fly-Tying.* Scribner's, New York, 1940.

Swisher, Doug, and Richards, Carl. *Fly Fishing Strategy.* Crown Publishers, New York, 1975.

Swisher, Doug, and Richards, Carl. *Selective Trout.* Crown Publishers, New York, 1971.

Talleur, Richard W. *Mastering the Art of Fly-Tying.* Stackpole Books, Harrisburg, 1979.

Taverner, Eric. *Fly-Tying for Trout.* Seeley Service, London, n.d.

Taverner, Eric. *Trout Fishing from All Angles.* Seeley Service, London, 1950.

Taylor, Samuel. *Angling in All Its Branches.* Longman and Rees, London, 1800.

Theakston, M. *British Angling Flies.* Harrison, Ripon . . . , 1883.

Tichborne, N. and B. *1986 New Zealand Trout Fly Calendar.* N. and B. Tichborne, Rotorua, 1985.

Trench, Charles Chenevix. *A History of Angling.* Follett, Chicago, 1974.

Turner, Brian, ed. *The Guide to Trout Fishing in Otago.* Otago Acclimatisation Society, 1985.

Turner, Eric Horsfall. *Angler's Cavalcade.* A. and C. Black, London, 1966.

Veniard, John. *Fly Dressers' Guide.* A. and C. Black, London, 1972.

Viner, A.B., ed. *Inland Waters of New Zealand.* Department of Scientific and Industrial Research, Wellington, 1987.

Vines, Sydney. *Frank Sawyer: Man of the Riverside.* Allen & Unwin, London, 1984.

Wade, Henry. *Halcyon.* Bell and Daldy, London, 1861.

Wakeford, Jacqueline. *Flytying Techniques.* Benn, London, 1980.

Walker, C.E. *Old Flies in New Dresses.* Lawrence and Bullen, London, 1898.

Walker, C.F. ed. *Angling Letters of G.E.M. Skues.* A. and C. Black, London, 1975.

Walker, C.F. *The Art of Chalk Stream Fishing.* Jenkins, London, 1968.

Walker, C.F. *Brown Trout and Dry Fly.* Seeley Service, London, 1955.

Walker, C.F. ed. *The Complete Fly-Fisher.* Barrie and Jenkins, London, 1972.

Walker, C.F. *Fly-Tying As An Art.* Jenkins, London, 1957.

Walker, C.F. *Lake Flies and Their Imitation.* Deutsch, London, 1983.

Walker, Dick. *Dick Walker's Modern Fly Dressings.* Benn, London, 1980.

Walton, Izaak, and Cotton, Charles. *The Complete Angler.* Navarre Society, London, 1925.

Weddell, Mike. *Ten of the Best New Zealand Trout Flies.* McIndoe, Dunedin, 1987.

Whitlock, Dave. *Guide to Aquatic Trout Foods.* Nick Lyons Books, New York, 1982.

Williams, A. Courtney. *A Dictionary of Trout Flies . . .* A. and C. Black, London, 1961.

Williams, A. Courtney. *Trout Flies: A Discussion and a Dictionary.* A. and C. Black, London, 1932.

Williamson, John. *The British Angler.* Hodges, London, 1740.

Williamson, Capt. T.E. *The Complete Angler's Vade-Mecum*. Payne and Mackinlay, London, 1808.

Winterbourn, Michael J. and Gregson, Katharine L.D. *Guide to the Aquatic Insects of New Zealand.* Entomological Society of New Zealand, Auckland, 1981.

Woolley, Roger. *Modern Trout Fly Dressing.* Fishing Gazette, London, 1932.

Wright, Leonard M., Jr. *Fishing the Dry Fly as a Living Insect.* Dutton, New York, 1972.

Wright, Leonard M., Jr. *Fly-Fishing Heresies.* Stoeger, New Jersey, 1978.

Zahner, Don, ed. *Fly Fisherman's Complete Guide to Fishing with the Fly Rod.* Ziff-Davis, New York, 1978.